M000011552

Taekwondo Kyorugi
Olympic Style Sparring

Taekwondo Kyorugi
Olympic Style Sparring

written by

Kuk Hyun Chung and Kyung Myung Lee

Translated and Edited by

Sang H. Kim

TP   Turtle Press   Hartford

TAEKWONDO KYORUGI

Copyright © 1994 Sang H. Kim. All rights reserved. Printed in the United States of America. No part of this book may be reproduced without written permission except in the case of brief quotations embodied in articles or reviews. For information, address Turtle Press, PO Box 290206, Wethersfield CT 06129-0206.

Photographs courtesy of: WTF
                             Kuk Hyun Chung
                             Kyung Myung Lee
                             Sang H. Kim

To contact the authors or to order additional copies of this book:
Turtle Press
401 Silas Deane Hwy
P.O. Box 290206
Wethersfield, CT 06129-0206
1-880-77-TURTL

Library of Congress Card Catalog Number 94-26035

ISBN 1-880336-05-7

First English Language Edition, Second Printing

Library of Congress Cataloguing-in-Publication Data

Chung, Kuk Hyun.
    [T' aekwondo kyŏrugi. English]
    Taekwondo Kyorugi : olympic style sparring / written by Kuk Hyun Chung and Kyung Myung Lee ; translated and edited by [i.e. edited] by Sang H. Kim. - - 1st English language ed.
        p.   cm.
    Includes bibliographical references and index.
    ISBN 1-880336-05-7
    1. T' aekwondo. 2. T' aekwondo - - xRules. 3. T' aekwondo - - Competitions. I. Lee, Kyung Myung. II. Kim, Sang H. III. Title. IV. Title: Olympic Style Sparring.
GV1114.9.C4813   1994
    796.8 - - dc20   94-26035

THE WORLD TAEKWONDO FEDERATION

635 YUKSAMDONG, KANGNAMKU
SEOUL, KOREA (135)
CABLE ADDRESS WORLD TAEKWONDO

A special message from President Un Yong Kim

June 1994

Taekwondo, which originated from Korea is now becoming a global sport. It is encouraging that this sport has become an official program of major multi-sport and continental games such as the Pan-Am Games, World Games, Goodwill Games, etc., making its value known to the whole world.

Athletes and coaches have to continuously train themselves for Taekwondo competition with both physical practice and study of the theories of taekwondo. Written materials for educating coaches and competitors are still not easy to access. I hope more documents of this nature will be published.

More research such as this should be made by Taekwondo practitioners and masters on the theorectical side of Taekwondo to increase its international popularity and make it an official Olympic sport. I commend Grandmaster Kyung Myung Lee, Master Sang Hwan Kim and Master Kuk Hyun Chung for their hard work toward the improvement of taekwondo and recommend this book be widely read by Taekwondo practitioners.

Dr. Un Yong Kim
President, WTF
Vice President, IOC

BEFORE YOU BEGIN

Exercises, advice and activities contained in this book are intended for elite level (professional) athletes and competitors. They are strenuous and may result in injury to the practitioner. As with all exercise programs, consult a physician before beginning.

Contents

Preface

Taekwondo originated over 2000 years ago in Korea. Now, in over 147 countries we hear the echoes of the dynamic kihap sound of taekwondo. Taekwondo is now a global sport and martial art. It has been contributing tremendously to the health and fitness of millions of practitioners for many years.

The World Taekwondo Federation, the official governing body of taekwondo, was formed in 1973. It was admitted into the General Association of the International Sports Federations (GAISF) and the International Olympic Committee (IOC) in 1980. Taekwondo debuted as an Olympic Demonstration Game in 1988 in Seoul, South Korea and was featured again in 1992 in Barcelona, Spain.

Even though taekwondo has become an international competitive sport, there is a distinct lack of contemporary educational materials for competitors, coaches, trainers and instructors. With the rapid innovations brought about by the internationalization of competitive taekwondo, continuing research and publication is necessary to allow competitors in every country access to modern taekwondo skills and strategy.

Taekwondo Kyorugi is a concise guide to competition for serious taekwondo competitors and instructors. The authors of this book have extensive experience in competing, coaching, and teaching at the highest levels of taekwondo. In writing this book, we have made great efforts to standardize the terminology and systemize the technical structure of competition training for the benefit of taekwondo competitors around the globe.

We hope *Taekwondo Kyorugi* will be a milestone for all taekwondo practitioners. Special thanks to Sung Hwan Chung and Sung Hee Lee and to Turtle Press which has greatly contributed to martial arts culture worldwide.

Spring 1994

Kyung Myung Lee
Sang Hwan Kim
Kuk Hyun Chung

Chapter 1:
Taekwondo
Competition

Taekwondo is a traditional Korean martial art and modern combat sport practiced all over the world. It has been developed, as in the cases of boxing, wrestling, fencing and judo, as a one-on-one combat sport. Taekwondo was an Olympic demonstration game in Seoul, Korea in 1988 and Barcelona, Spain in 1992, with eight weight divisions.

Taekwondo literally consists of three words:

Tae　　(태) means a system of foot techniques
Kwon (권) means a system of hand techniques
Do　　(도) means the art of experiencing the
　　　　　　ultimate being through physical and
　　　　　　metaphysical enlightenment

Taekwondo practitioners can develop strong physical fitness and mental strength through basic techniques, poomse (form), Kyukpa (breaking), Machuo Kyorugi (arranged sparring), and Jayu Kyorugi (free sparring). Through practicing the spectrum of taekwondo skills the practitioner can prepare himself not only for competition but also for any life-threatening situations.

Taekwondo is a total fitness program. If *Taekwon* denotes the external form of the art, *Do* connotes the internal essence. The essence of Taekwondo begins from the spirit of martial arts. It is a way of improving the self through constant internal struggles between the negative self and the positive one.

To achieve the highest state of the mind, it is necessary for taekwondo practitioners to experience constant battles between the real self and the illusive self, the right way and the wrong way. To help further this process, meditation is frequently used. Meditation is an essential element in attaining the highest state of mind. The main goal of meditation is the attainment of enlightenment. The result of this combination of physical and mental training is the cultivation of character and the discovery of the ideal path in life. The ultimate answer to what Taekwondo is can be defined as a *philosophical activity through which the practitioner can attain the highest level of unity of the body, mind, and spirit.*

"The ultimate winner is the one who can conquer himself. Kyorugi is a fight within the self. The one who can win himself can eventually win over the opponent."

Kyorugi and Competition

Kyorugi is an actual fight between two competitors using the offensive and defensive skills acquired through the practice of Taekwondo. There are two types of Kyorugi as defined by the degree of limitation of the skills allowed. They are machuo kyorugi (arranged sparring) and jayu kyorugi (free sparring). Jayu kyorugi is the form of sparring that is implemented in Taekwondo competition.

Valid techniques for scoring points in competition include a variety of punching and kicking skills. The punch can be used only to the trunk (areas covered by the chest guard) and kicking techniques can be executed to the face (head, in front of the ears) and trunk (areas covered by the chest guard). Any technique below the belt is prohibited. One point is awarded to a technique that is delivered accurately on a legal area with the proper amount of power. To score a valid point, an attack must be acknowledged by two or more judges. The winner is decided by points or knock out. If case of a tie, the winner is decided by the rule of superiority.

Illegal techniques and behavior are penalized by a warning (kyung-go) or deduction of a point (gam-jeom). The accumulation of two warnings by a competitor results in the deduction of one point. The competitor who accumulates three deduction points, by kyung-go or gam-jeom penalties, throughout the match is automatically disqualified.

Most of the vital points of the legal target areas are shielded by protection gear worn by the competitors. It is mandatory for all competitors to wear head gear, a chest protector, shin guards, forearm guards, and a groin protector to prevent potential injuries.

Taekwondo competition takes place on the 26' x 26' mat between two competitors identified by the color of their chest protectors as blue (chung) and red (hong). Competitors are divided by weight and gender into sixteen divisions. A standard international match consists of three rounds of three minutes with a one minute break between rounds. The match is officiated by a head of court, a referee, 4 corner judges, a timekeeper, and a recorder.

The Spirit of Competition

As in the Olympic slogan of "Faster, Higher, and Stronger," taekwondo competition encourages competitors to improve the level of human capacity. Taekwondo competition is a form of education that takes place through the practice of skills and their application in competition, based on traditional values. The fundamental significance of taekwondo competition lies in the fact that the competition ring provides a venue where following the rules and doing one's best are rewarded. The site of competition is a place to learn the way to achieve harmony and perfection of the mind, body and spirit through the discovery of true self. This is possible through the struggle within self and against the opponent.

Competition is a method of developing the full potential of the human body, both physically and technically. Taekwondo competition pursues the development and integration of fitness, technique and strategy as well as a sense of humility and sportsmanship.

The ultimate ideal of taekwondo practice is to achieve a state of mind in which the performer is acutely aware of the endlessly changing competition environment and can effortlessly react to such changes. This state of mind becomes possible through the mastery of a broad range of offensive and defensive taekwondo skills.

Development of Competition

From ancient times, taekwondo has been practiced as a form of self-defense on both the individual and national levels. During the Japanese colonial period in Korea (1910-1945), the Japanese government prohibited traditional Korean martial arts training to prevent antigovernment uprising by the Korean people. After liberation from the Japanese on August 15, 1945, the elders of the Korean martial arts community met to revive the traditional, preoccupation arts. Because of these efforts, the Korea Taekwondo Association (KTA) was formed in 1961.

In 1963, taekwondo was accepted as an official event in the 43rd National Athletic Festival marking the official debut of taekwondo as a national sport. Since the early 1960's, many Korean taekwondo instructors have taken up residence throughout the world, promoting taekwondo in their new home countries. Because of this, taekwondo has enjoyed global popularity as an international sport. This trend has also been marked by the ascent of kyorugi as the main area of practice for taekwondo competitors.

In 1973, the first World Taekwondo Championship was held in Seoul, Korea with eighteen participating countries. At this time, the World Taekwondo Federation (WTF) was formed to support the worldwide taekwondo movement in a more structured way. Since 1973, the World Taekwondo Championship has been held every two years, with 1987 marking the first time women's competition divisions were included.

The headquarters of the WTF is located at Kukkiwon in Seoul, Korea. The WTF is the official international governing body for taekwondo and has a membership of over 145 countries. It is now recognized by both the International Olympic Committee (IOC) and the General Association of the International Sports Federations (GAISF). Under the auspices of these and other regional organizations, taekwondo is included in many international, regional and national sporting events.

Timeline of Modern Taekwondo

Sept. 16, 1961	Korea Taekwondo Association (KTA) formed
Feb. 23, 1963	Taekwondo accepted into Korea Athletic Assoc.
Nov. 30, 1972	Kukkiwon, headquarters of taekwondo, built
May 25, 1973	1st Men's World Taekwondo Championship
May 28, 1973	World Taekwondo Federation (WTF) formed
Oct. 18, 1974	1st Asian Taekwondo Championship held
Oct. 5, 1975	Recognized by GAISF
Apr. 9, 1976	Recognized by Conseil Internationale du Sports Militaire (CISM)
July 17, 1980	Recognized by International Olympic Committee (IOC)
July 3, 1986	1st World Cup Taekwondo Championship
Sept. 30, 1986	Accepted as an official sport in Asian Games
Nov. 29, 1986	1st World Collegiate Taekwondo Championship
Aug. 9, 1987	Accepted as an official sport in Pan-Am Games
Oct. 7, 1987	1st Women's World Taekwondo Championship
Sept. 17, 1988	Olympic demonstration games held, Korea
July. 30, 1992	Olympic demonstration games held, Spain

Taekwondo demonstration at the 1988 Olympic Games in Seoul

Official International Taekwondo Events

International Championships

- World Taekwondo Championships
- World Cup
- FISU (World Collegiate Championship)
- CISM (World Military Championship)

Regional Championships

- Asian Taekwondo Championship
- European Taekwondo Championship
- Pan-Am Taekwondo Championship
- African Taekwondo Championship
- Southeast Asian Taekwondo Championship
- Middle Eastern Taekwondo Championship
- Mediterranean Cup Taekwondo Championship

Multi-sport/Continental Championships

- Olympic Demonstration Games (1988, 1992)
- World Games
- Pan-Am Games
- Central American Sports Games
- Caribbean Games
- All-Africa Games
- Asian Games (1986, 1994)
- Southeast Asian Games
- South American Games
- Goodwill Games

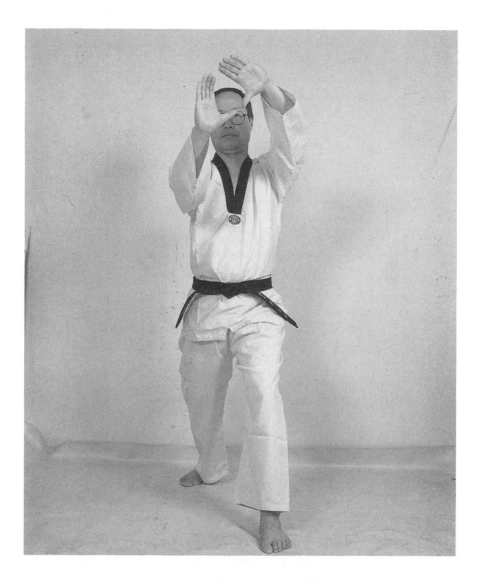

Grandmaster Kyung Myung Lee

Chapter 2:
Competition Skills

Technical proficiency in taekwondo competition cannot be attained by chance. It can only be achieved through the consistent effort of the competitor and his or her coach, trainer or instructor. Taekwondo competition is designed to be a direct contest of skills between two opponents in which the outcome appears to be determined by the power and accuracy of each competitor's skills.

However, at the highest levels of competition, an acute sense of strategy and discerning technique selection are required to outmaneuver and defeat the opponent. Based on the basic skills of taekwondo, each competitor, along with his or her coach, must develop a unique method of attack and counterattack that is best suited to his or her style.

Since the ultimate goal of competition is to defeat the opponent, each competitor must cultivate certain characteristics that are essential for achieving victory. The most fundamental attributes of every competitor include skillful technique, physical and mental fitness, strategy, agility and innate athleticism. Beyond these fundamentals, perennial champions demonstrate the consistent ability to improve and adapt their skills and strategy and to perform well under pressure.

Components of a Competitor

Limited ability factors

1. General factors
    a. speed
    b. flexibility
    c. coordination

2. Athletic skill factors
    a. offense skills
    b. countering skills
    c. footwork

3. Mental factors
    a. motivation
    b. self-awareness
    c. self-control
    d. concentration
    e. strategy

Decisive ability factors

1. Mental factors
    a. general intellect
    b. mental training and others

2. General physical factors
    a. endurance
    b. agility
    c. power

3. Physical structural factors
    a. symmetry
    b. height

Techniques

Taekwondo techniques can be viewed as a means of resolving the situations presented in competition. Through proper analysis of each situation, the competitor can select and apply the correct attack or counterattack, resulting in the neutralization of the opponent and thereby achieving the necessary objective. The ability to size up and quickly react to the given situation is very important in advancing in competition.

To be able to apply the necessary skills, each skill must be thoroughly understood through a process of learning, practicing and eventually mastering it. At the advanced level, taekwondo skills become increasingly complex and require a highly specialized level of fitness especially concerning flexibility, power, coordination, agility and reflexes.

There are many competition skills available to the taekwondo competitor. The most commonly used skills include:

1. Punching (jirugi) using the two foreknuckles
   a. straight middle punch
   b. angular middle punch

2. Kicking (chagi) using the foot below the ankle
   a. roundhouse kick
   b. back kick
   c. axe kick
   d. spin whip kick
   e. whip kick
   f. side kick
   g. front kick
   h. turning kick

3. Footwork (baljitgi) through strategic stepping
   a. forward footwork
   b. backward footwork
   c. lateral footwork

    d. turning footwork
    e. drawing footwork

4. Blocking (maki) using the hand and arm
    a. direct block
    b. indirect block

5. Feinting (sogimsu) using deceptive gestures
    a. footwork feinting
    b. body feinting
    c. motion feinting

The difference between competition taekwondo and martial taekwondo lies in the limitations placed on the range of applicable skills. In competition, the legal targets, for which the competitor may be awarded a point, include the head and trunk (see *Chapter 9: Competition Rules* for specific target areas). Therefore, the competitor must always be conscious of these targets and select techniques which result in the scoring of a point against such targets.

1. Fighting Stance (Kyorumsae)

Kyorumsae is an abbreviation of kyorugi and jasae. Kyorugi means fighting or sparring and jasae means stance. Kyorumsae, therefore, indicates the position the fighter assumes in preparation to fight.

The competitor must practice a correct fighting stance from the early stages of training. The appearance of the fighting stance differs according to the individual fighter's body structure and personal preference. Most fighting stances change according to the situation, including whether the fighter is in an offensive or defensive posture and whether he is preparing to move or has just finished a movement.

A. The components of a good fighting stance

1) Flexibility
A good stance allows for smooth, continuous movement by maintaining flexibility of posture.

2) Natural body posture
A good stance allows the body to act and react spontaneously, without undue hindrance.

3) Agility
A good stance allows for movement in any direction at split second intervals.

4) Base
A good stance requires a wide enough base (the distance between the feet) to maintain balance in movement and at rest.

5) Center of gravity
A good stance maintains the proper placement of the center of gravity, higher for rapid movements and lower for powerful movements.

6) Concealment
A good stance allows the fighter to hide the intention and initiation of offensive movements.

B. Types of fighting stance

1) Standard fighting stance (kyorumsae)

The standard fighting stance, also called the front fighting stance, is the most fundamental stance in sparring. Based on the position of the rear foot, the standard stance is classified as either right handed or left handed. When the right foot is in the rear, it is a right handed stance and when the left foot is in the rear, it is a left handed stance. To make the standard fighting stance, position your feet at 1½ or 2 times your regular stride and turn your body approximately 45° to the side. From this stance, the execution of every taekwondo technique is possible.

2) Side fighting stance (yup-kyorumsae)

The side fighting stance is a variation of the standard fighting stance. The distance between the feet is slightly wider and the body is turned completely to the side. Side fighting stance is good for executing side kick and back kick.

3) Low fighting stance (natchoomsae)

The low fighting stance is second variation of the standard fighting stance. The distance between the feet is the same as in the side fighting stance and the body position is between that of the standard and side stances. The knees are bent lower than in the other stances and the upper body can lean slightly forward. Low fighting stance is good for counterattacking, especially with roundhouse kick and spin whip kick.

Standard fighting stance

Side fighting stance

Low fighting stance

C. Stance as related to the opponent

When considering the relationship of the fighters' stances, there are two possible configurations, open stance and closed stance.

1) Open stance (yullimsae)

Open stance suggests that the targets of the head and trunk are "open" to the opponent. Open stance is created when one fighter is in a left handed stance and the other is in a right handed stance.

2) Closed stance (datchimsae)

Closed stance suggests that the targets of the opponent are hidden or "closed" to attack. Closed stance is created when both fighters concurrently assume a right handed or left handed stance.

2. Fundamental Offense Techniques

The offensive arsenal of taekwondo skills is made up of kicks and punches. Because of their longer attacking range and greater potential for power, kicks are the preferred attacks of taekwondo fighters. In traditional taekwondo, impacting with the ball, edge or heel of the foot is the prescribed method of kicking. However, in sport taekwondo the instep and bottom of the foot are the primary weapons for kicking.

1) Roundhouse kick (dollyo-chagi)

The roundhouse kick is the most frequently used kick in taekwondo because of its high rate of accuracy and simplicity. To execute the roundhouse kick, first chamber the knee and simultaneously pivot 180° on the supporting leg. Using the instep, strike to the face, stomach or rib/kidney area.

2) Back kick (dui-chagi)

Back kick is preferred for counterattacking when there is less risk in turning the back to the opponent. In initiative attacking, the back kick should be long and penetrating, while for counterattacking it must be short and quick. To execute the back kick, pivot on the front foot while chambering the back leg. Quickly look over the turning shoulder at the opponent's movement. Turn the body slightly toward the target while the kicking foot passes by the supporting knee in a direct line to the target. Keep the upper body erect during the execution for maximum efficiency. The target for back kick is the trunk.

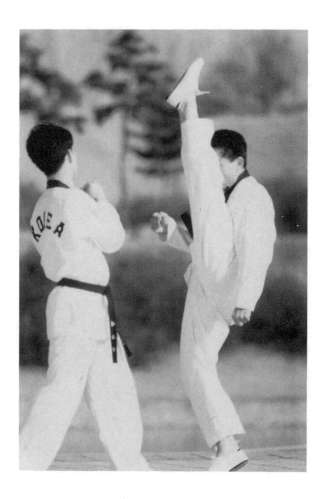

3) Axe kick (naeryo-chagi)

Axe kick has two main variations, bent knee kicking and straight knee kicking. To execute the bent knee axe kick, chamber the knee and unfold it in a downward direction, beginning at the highest point of the kicking trajectory. To execute the straight knee axe kick, lift the leg straight up at a slightly off center angle and drop it on the target. Both kicks can be used as inside kicking or outside kicking, defined by the relative position of your leg to the opponent's body. The striking surface of the foot is the sole or heel and the target is the face.

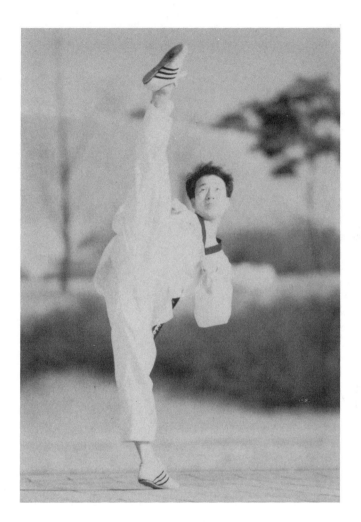

4) Whip kick (hooryo-chagi)

The whip kick can be executed with the lead or rear leg. For the lead leg whip kick, chamber the leg in front of the body and release it in a circular motion. For the rear leg whip kick, the body must first turn 180 degrees to chamber the leg in front. The sole of the foot is used to strike the face.

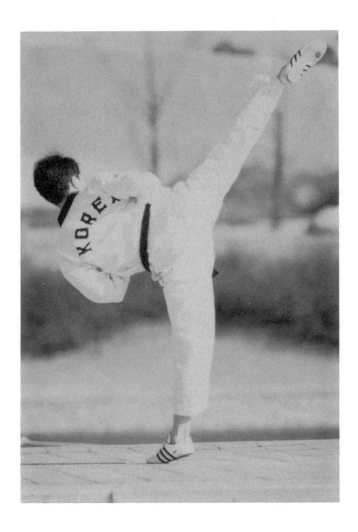

5) Spin whip kick (dui-hooryo-chagi)

The spin whip kick must be executed quickly and accurately to be efficient and powerful. To execute the spin whip kick, pivot on the front leg and chamber the rear leg. As the body spins around, release the kicking leg in a circular motion. During the spinning movement, quickly look at opponent over the turning shoulder. The sole of the foot is used to strike the face.

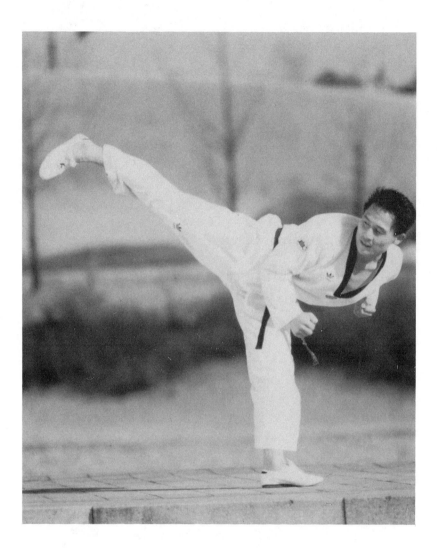

6) Side kick (yup-chagi)

The side kick is most effective when used as a front leg attack from the side stance. Chamber the leg and thrust it toward the target in a direct linear movement. The sole or edge of the foot is used to strike the trunk.

7) Pushing kick (mirro-chagi)

The pushing kick is used as a feint or a setup before the main attack. Pushing kick can be executed with the rear leg or the lead leg. Chamber the kicking knee slightly and quickly push toward the waist of the opponent with the sole of the foot.

8) Punch (jirugi)

Punching is used as a counterattack or as a tool to create space for follow-up kicks. When the push is accurately and powerfully delivered by the foreknuckles of the fist to the opponent's trunk it can score a point.

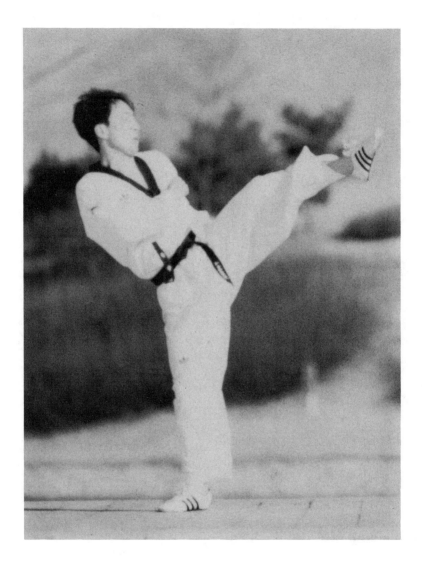

9) Front kick (ahp-chagi)

The front kick is rarely used in competition because the potential for injury to the ball of the foot and toes is great. To execute the front kick, chamber the knee and simultaneously thrust the foot to the target in a linear motion. The ball of the foot is used to strike the trunk and face.

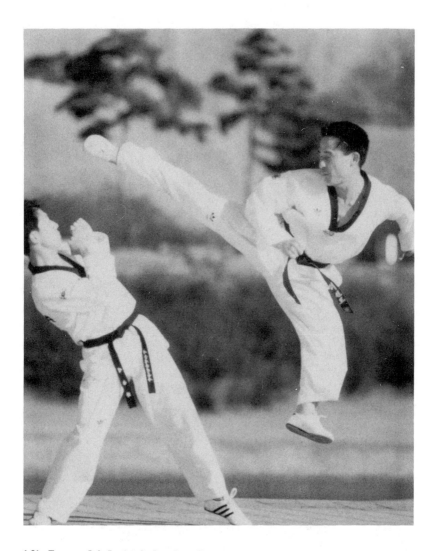

10) Jump kick (tuiuh-chagi)

All of the basic kicking skills of taekwondo can be executed as jumping kicks as well. However, the longer you stay in the air while jumping, the more opportunity you provide the opponent for a counterattack. In competition, jumping kicks are generally used as short counterattacking techniques. When employed as an initiative attack, the jump is used to close the distance and penetrate the opponent's defenses rather than to achieve height.

11) Single leg combination kick (eeuh-chagi)

A single leg combination kick, two kicks with the same leg, requires great speed and technical proficiency. The striking surface and targets vary according to the type of kick. Examples of single leg combination kicks include middle section roundhouse kick followed by high section roundhouse kick and axe kick followed by side kick.

12) Double kick (doobal-dangsung-chagi)

A combination kick is executed by jumping and performing two kicks, one with each leg, before landing. It requires speed and advanced technical proficiency. The striking surface and target can vary with the type of kicks used. The two kicks may be the same type (e.g., two roundhouse kicks) or different (e.g. twisting kick and side kick).

3. Footwork (jitgi)

Footwork is an indirect skill used to set up a scoring technique. Footwork changes according to the opponent's stance, position, distance and the situation. The goals of footwork are:
1. to disrupt the opponent's offensive strategy
2. to avoid being attacked
3. to create a weakness in the opponent's movements
4. to create an opening in the opponent's defense
5. to launch an accurate and timely attack.

Tips for successful footwork:
1. shift the body smoothly and lightly
2. synchronize the entire body as one unit
3. maintain equilibrium throughout every movement
4. adapt the stance according to the technique

An example of footwork combined with kicking: slide forward and follow with roundhouse kick to the midsection.

Types of Footwork

Using a variety of footwork is an essential skill in taekwondo. Footwork is classified into five types according to the direction and structure of movement of the feet.

1) Forward footwork (naga-jitgi)

There are two types of forward footwork: *forward step*, in which the rear foot steps forward and the front foot acts as pivot and *forward slide*, in which both feet slide forward maintaining the same stance. The function of forward footwork is to shorten the distance to the opponent and secure the position that is best for attacking. Forward footwork is best followed by roundhouse kick or back kick.

2) Backward footwork (moollo-jitgi)

There are two types of backward footwork: *backward step*, in which the front foot steps back and the rear foot acts as pivot and *backward slide*, in which both feet slide backward maintaining the same stance. Backward footwork is best followed by round-house kick, back kick, and spin whip kick.

3) Lateral footwork (beekyo-jitgi)

There are two types of lateral footwork: *lateral pivot*, in which the rear foot moves at a forty-five degree angle to right or left while the front foot acts as pivot and *lateral slide*, in which both feet simultaneously slide to the right or left maintaining the same stance. Lateral footwork is best followed by an immediate counterattack, such as a roundhouse kick, axe kick or turn kick.

4) Turning footwork (dwidora-jitgi)

Turning footwork indicates turning the body 180° forward to the posterior side by moving the rear foot and using the front foot as a pivot. The best techniques for turning are roundhouse, axe kick and whip kick.

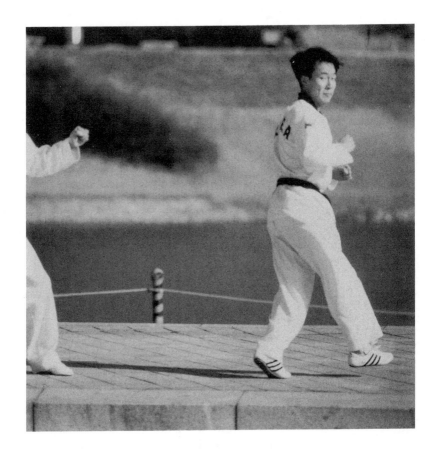

An example of turning footwork.

5) Drawing footwork (kulro-jitgi)

There are two types of drawing footwork: the *front foot draw* in which the front foot is drawn along the ground toward the rear foot and *rear foot draw* in which the rear foot is drawn along the ground toward the front foot. Front drawing is especially effective when combined with a simultaneous rear leg round-house kick. Other kicks combined with drawing footwork are roundhouse kick, axe kick and whip kick.

Sample combinations of footwork and kicking

Footwork	Kick	Target	Foot
Forward footwork	back kick roundhouse spin whip axe kick	trunk trunk/face face face	front/back " " "
Backward footwork	back kick roundhouse spin whip	trunk trunk/face face	front/back " "
Lateral footwork	roundhouse axe kick	trunk/face face	back "
Turning footwork	roundhouse whip kick spin whip	trunk/face face face	front " "
Drawing footwork	axe kick whip kick roundhouse	face face trunk/face	front " "

4. Combination Skills

A combination is a continuous attack that is comprised of at least two techniques. Combinations, like other skills, are largely developed based on personal style and preference. Beyond personal preference, there are several basic principles behind the development of combination techniques. First, the competitor must master single techniques such as roundhouse kick or back kick. Next, he must be able to combine these skills smoothly and apply them with the required footwork and feinting skills.

Examples of common combinations:
- a. right foot roundhouse kick to the trunk, left foot roundhouse kick to the face
- b. right foot roundhouse kick to the trunk, left foot back kick to the trunk
- c. right foot roundhouse kick to the trunk, left foot roundhouse kick to the trunk
- d. left foot turn kick to the trunk, right foot back kick to the trunk
- e. left foot axe kick to the face, right foot roundhouse kick to the trunk

Combination A: Right foot roundhouse kick followed by left foot roundhouse kick

5. Defense Techniques

There are two types of defensive skills in taekwondo: direct defense and indirect defense. **Direct defense** means blocking a kick to the head or body by covering potential targets with the arm. An effective block prevents the opponent from scoring a point. There are two basic types of blocks: single block in which the forearm is used to cover the trunk or head area and double block in which one arm comes up to cover the head and the other drops to cover the trunk.

Indirect defense means avoiding an attack by moving out of its path using footwork or a change of stance. Indirect defense skills are usually followed by a counterattack. Counterattacking right after avoiding an attack is one of the most effective means of scoring in taekwondo competition.

A double block used against a high section roundhouse kick.

6. Feinting Skills

A feint is an intentionally deceptive movement, intended to draw the opponent's attack and leave him open to a predetermined counterattack. The key to feinting is to deceive the opponent psychologically and cause him to misjudge the situation. A common feint is to make a front leg kicking motion and attack with a rear leg roundhouse kick or back kick.

Other types of feints are created through:
  a. body gestures that cause the opponent to lose his balance
  b. footwork that makes the opponent lose his sense of distance
  c. drawing that falsely causes the opponent to think there is a target open for him to attack easily.

The attacker uses a pushing kick to disrupt his opponent's distance and balance and then follows up with a jumping back kick to score.

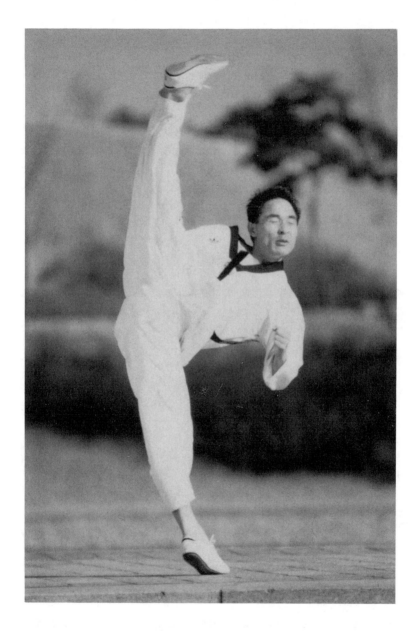

Master Kuk Hyung Chung

Chapter 3: Strategies

Strategy is a method to defeat the opponent through analysis of the situation, judgment of the available options and immediate execution of the most appropriate action. The purpose of using strategy is to manage the course of the match while conserving energy and moving wisely.

To execute an effective strategy in the match the fighter must be thoroughly familiar with the rules and regulations of the game, as well as the strategies in use by the current top international fighters, and have mastered fundamental skills that work in every situation. In the ring, the fighter also must be able to rely on his coach to evaluate the opponent and formulate strategy based on this evaluation.

Competition taekwondo is a game of strategy. The result of the match often hinges on the strategic proficiency of the competitors.

❖ 3 Considerations for Competition Strategy

1) *Technical structure and variations according to the competition rules.* Every competitor must be able to win within the established framework of the competition rules. He must create unique offensive combinations designed to score points while avoiding penalties.

2) *Economical use of energy over the duration of the match.* A fighter must plan his strategy over the course of the full nine minutes of the match. He must clearly decide when it is appropriate to conserve energy and when it is necessary to press the opponent.

3) *Judicial application of feinting skills.* Feinting should be used wisely and sparingly, so as not to be detected by the opponent.

The following process is necessary for the accurate formulation (psychological) and execution (physical) of strategy:

1. **Psychological formulation of strategy**
   a. concentration (attention to the opponent's every action)
   b. information collection (accumulation of information)
   c. data selection (sorting of the important information)
   d. analysis of the situation (projection of future events)
   e. decision making (selection of appropriate action)
   f. immediate execution (implementation of chosen action)

2. **Physical execution of strategy**
   g. adaptation (change of techniques according to situation)
   h. economic distribution of energy (conservation and assertion of energy at the proper time)
   i. timing (attack/defend appropriately)
   j. execution of plan (carry out planned strategy)
   k. score management (score enough points to win)

Offensive Strategy

Offense, in taekwondo competition, is the strategic application of skills to the target area of the opponent. It is most commonly applied with forward footwork and explosive movements. To be successful, offensive skills must be executed with good timing and an accurate sense of distance.

There are three methods of offense: direct attack, indirect attack and counterattack. A direct attack is an initiative attack, an indirect attack is a deceptive attack and a counterattack is a reflexive attack.

Direct attack

There are three types of direct attacks according to the *distance* and *stance* of the opponent.

1. The first is an **in-place attack** where the distance to the opponent is perfect for a single kicking attack and no footwork or deception is required.

2. The second is an **incline attack** where the distance is slightly beyond the reach of an in-place attack. Therefore the competitor must shift his body forward without moving his feet, and launch the attack from the inclined position. Timing, distance and speed are essential.

3. The third is a **sliding attack** where the distance is even greater than that of the incline attack. The competitor must slide his front foot in as he shifts his body weight forward to attack. Speed is essential for covering the distance in a sliding attack. For maximum efficiency, the competitor must execute the technique before the opponent recognizes his intention.

Indirect attack

There are three types of indirect attack: feinting, cutting and footwork.

1. **Feinting**: To create an opening, feint first and then attack according to the opponent's reaction.

2. **Cutting**: Cut the opponent's attacking movement and follow with a counterattack.

3. **Footwork**: According to the distance and stance of the opponent, initiate with footwork and attack.

Counterattack

There are two types of counter attacks: direct and indirect.

1. A **direct counterattack** means countering the opponent's attack without changing position. Speed, agility and fortitude are important for direct counterattacking.

2. An **indirect counterattack** means avoiding the opponent's attack with footwork and then following with a counterattack.

Summary of Offensive Options:

1. Direct Attack
   - a. in-place attack
   - b. incline attack
   - c. sliding attack
2. Indirect Attack
   - a. feinting
   - b. cutting
   - c. drawing
3. Counterattack
   - a. direct
   - b. indirect

Assessing the Opponent

The goal of opponent assessment is to determine the opponent's:
    a. strategy
    b. technical skill
    c. mentality
    d. physical condition

This can be achieved by noting the following components of the opponent:
    a. height
    b. stance
    c. fighting style
          - infighter or outfighter
          - attacker or counterattacker
    d. favorite skill
    e. psychological condition
    f. strength and weakness

Closing the distance with direct attack.

Statistics for Formulating a Successful Strategy

Conclusions from Master Sang Jin Han, "Research of Frequency and Scoring Rate of Individual Skills of Taekwondo Competition," 1993 and Master Jae Bong Lee, "Analytical Research into Scoring Rate of Initiative Attack and Counter Attack of Taekwondo Competition," 1993

1. The **single attack** is used most frequently in competition because it can be executed from a stable stance.

2. A **counterattack** is good for scoring points because the competitor can wait for the perfect opportunity and attack while the opponent is off guard.

3. **Attacking** is more advantageous in competition because the rule of superiority states that in a tie, the more aggressive fighter wins.

4. **Counterattacking** has the highest success rate of any type of attack in terms of scoring points.

5. The **most frequently used kicks**, in descending order, are: roundhouse kick to the trunk, back kick to the trunk, axe kick to the face, roundhouse kick to the face, pushing kick to the trunk, punching to the trunk, spin whip kick to the face, front kick to the trunk, and side kick to the trunk.

6. The **kicks that score** most frequently, in descending order, are: roundhouse kick to the trunk, back kick to the trunk, roundhouse kick to the face, axe kick to the face, axe kick to the trunk, and spin whip kick to the face.

7. The kicks with the **highest of percentage of points** scored, (ratio of points scored to frequency of use) in descending order, are: back kick to trunk, roundhouse kick to face, roundhouse kick to the body, axe kick to the face, spin whip kick to the face, and pushing kick to the trunk.

8. The **most productive rounds** for scoring, in descending order, are: third round, second round, and first round.

Chapter 4:
Professional
Kyorugi Training

The goal of professional kyorugi training is to practice and perfect selected strategic techniques for use in actual competition. Professional training takes the competitor beyond the practice of basic movements and into the direct, successful application of skills as a whole unit. The goal of training is technical improvement and overall skill integration. This training must be done consistently throughout the competition preparation and competition season and should be geared toward maximum gains in the minimum amount of time.

Professional skill drills are a means of mastering the direct application of previously acquired techniques and strategy. The main focus of the training is the repeated drilling of the most frequently used advanced skills and their applications. The type of techniques vary according to the level of the physical and mental condition of the competitor.

There are five fundamental guidelines for implementing professional skill drills:

a. always use them at the beginning of the workout

b. schedule intensive repetition of skills

c. execute accurately with maximum power and speed

d. give full focus and conscious attention to performance

e. maintain supplementary physical training

Examples of Professional Skill Drills

1. Roundhouse kick (target: trunk)

- in-place rear leg roundhouse kick
- in-place multiple roundhouse kicks
- lead foot step in, roundhouse kick
- quick step, lead leg roundhouse kick
- in-place double roundhouse kick
- rear foot step back, double roundhouse kick
- in-place switch stance, roundhouse kick
- lead leg pushing kick, rear roundhouse kick
- rear leg roundhouse kick, return to same stance, same leg roundhouse kick
- lead leg feint, double roundhouse kick
- 360° spin (lead foot pivot), in-place roundhouse kick
- lead leg feint, front step in, roundhouse kick
- turn and side step, roundhouse kick
- switch stance, lead foot draw and roundhouse kick
- rear foot draw, roundhouse kick
- switch stance, lead leg roundhouse kick (trunk is fixed)

In-place, rear leg roundhouse kick

In-place, double roundhouse kick

2. Roundhouse kick (target: face)

- in-place roundhouse kick
- lead foot step in, roundhouse kick
- front foot draw, roundhouse kick
- rear hand punch, roundhouse kick

Lead foot step in, roundhouse kick

3. Back kick (target: trunk)

- in-place back kick
- lead foot step in, back kick
- switch stance, back kick
- rear foot step in, jumping back kick

In-place back kick

Rear foot step in, jumping back kick

4. Axe kick (target: face)

- rear leg axe kick
- lead leg axe kick, slide forward, lead leg axe kick
- lead leg jumping axe kick
- lead leg feint, simultaneous rear leg jump axe kick
- rear foot step back, lead leg axe kick

Lead leg jumping axe kick

5. Spin whip kick (target: face)

- in-place spin whip kick
- lead foot step in, spin whip kick
- slide back, spin whip kick
- in-place jumping spin whip kick
- step on the opponent's body, jumping spin whip kick

Step on the opponent's body, jumping spin whip kick

6. Counterattack

- slide back, roundhouse kick
- rear foot step back, lead leg roundhouse kick to face
- in-place lead leg roundhouse kick
- in-place lead leg axe kick
- slide back, double roundhouse kick
- in-place back kick
- in-place jumping back kick
- in-place spin whip kick
- in-place jumping spin whip kick
- slide back, jumping turn kick

In-place jumping spin whip kick

Independent Training

When practicing alone, every technique can be practiced singularly or in combination, at the individual's pace. The diverse stances and footwork of taekwondo can be combined with kicking skills, independently or in combinations, without the influence of a partner. By practicing independently, the fighter can practice a specific drill of his own rhythm, speed, skill level and physical condition. This type of practice is effective for perfecting advanced skills.

Examples of independent training include:

1. **Image training**, in which the fighter practices against an imaginary opponent, is good for developing control of advanced skills, fine motor coordination, technical creativity and accurate self-evaluation.
2. **Audio or visual cue training**, in which the fighter responds to predetermined signals or commands, develops quick reflexes.
3. **Fixed target or mirror practice**, using the heavy bag or mirror, develops accuracy.

Training with a Partner

Training with a partner takes place with a limited but active execution of skills according to the varying movements of a partner. Techniques must be performed differently according to the opponent's execution of his techniques and strategy. The competitor must strive for the accurate performance of skills with attentiveness.

Partner training is a direct method of improving the actual competition ability. There are two types of partner training according to the method and goals of training: basic skill drills and strategy training.

1. Basic skill drills

To improve the internal sense of timing, distance and accuracy of techniques, practice with a partner is essential. To develop balance and variety in the offensive arsenal, every skill must be practiced equally with the right and left sides of the body.

Basic skill drills are practiced in pairs. There are **four basic methods of drilling** the competitors: *practice by command* or signals, *free practice* with feinting, *speed and agility practice* and *endurance practice*. All of the drills can be executed in place, moving forward, moving backward or in zigzag patterns. It is best to rotate partners regularly to enhance the competitors' adaptability to different types of opponents. Drills also can be practiced using hand targets for accuracy.

Example A: Hand skill counterattacking drills

The following drills are practiced to develop close distance counterattacking skills:

a. In open stance, the attacker executes rear leg roundhouse kick to the trunk of the defender. The defender uses a rear forearm low block and counters with a lead hand punch to the trunk of the attacker.

b. In closed stance, the attacker executes a rear leg roundhouse kick to the trunk of the defender. The defender uses a lead forearm low block and counters with a rear hand punch to the trunk.

c. In closed stance, the attacker executes rear leg round-house kick to the face of the defender. The defender uses a lead arm outside high section block and counters with a rear hand punch to the trunk.

Example B: Kicking counterattack drills

The following drills are practiced to develop middle distance counterattacking skills:

a. In closed stance, the attacker executes rear leg round-house kick to the trunk of the defender. The defender counters with an in-place rear leg roundhouse kick to the trunk.

b. In closed stance, the attacker executes rear leg axe kick to the trunk of the defender. The defender counters with an in-place rear leg roundhouse kick to the trunk.

c. In open stance, the attacker executes rear leg roundhouse kick to the trunk of the defender. The defender counters with an in-place back kick to the trunk.

d. In closed stance, the attacker executes rear leg spin whip kick to the face of the defender. The defender counters with a lead leg roundhouse kick to the trunk.

e. In closed stance, the attacker executes rear leg back kick to the trunk of the defender. The defender counters with a back slide, rear leg roundhouse kick to the trunk.

Example C: Footwork counterattacking drills

The following chart lists sample drills to be practiced with a partner in basic training to develop general attacking and counterattacking skills. *Attacker* indicates the actions of the attacking partner and *Defender* indicates the response of the counterattacking partner. *Footwork* indicates the footwork to be executed by the defender before kicking.

Attacker	Defender	Footwork (defender)
roundhouse	roundhouse kick	backward diagonal step
pushing kick	back kick	"
back kick	spin whip kick	"
side kick	whip kick	"
front kick	side kick	"
	front kick	"
axe kick	roundhouse kick	lead foot draw
spin whip	whip kick	forward step
back kick	pushing kick	backward step
push kick	side kick	lead foot draw
	back kick	lead foot draw

The attacker executes a roundhouse kick. The defender counters with a roundhouse kick.

Example D: Combined Counterattacking skills **

Attack	Stance	Counter	Footwork	Hand/Foot
Round-house kick	open " closed " " "	back kick punch axe kick spin whip roundhouse whip kick	side step " " " " "	rear lead rear " " "
Back Kick	both "	roundhouse axe kick	side step "	rear "
Axe Kick	both closed closed	roundhouse " "	side step back step draw	rear " rear
Spin Whip	closed "	roundhouse "	side step turn back	rear lead
Whip Kick	open closed	roundhouse back kick	back step "	rear "
Punch	open "	back kick spin whip	in place "	rear "

** All attacking skills are executed with the rear leg or hand.

2. Strategic Skill Drills

Strategic skill drills are professional training methods to perfect necessary skills through consistent repetitive training. Strategic thinking, timing, adaptability, and the ability to execute advanced skills are the key components in this training. There are *four types of strategic skill drills*:

 a. training without protection gear
 b. training with protection gear
 c. training with supplementary equipment (targets)
 d. individual special skill training using a heavy bag

Types of strategic training according to fighting stance:

1. Closed stance

 a. Kicking Attacks

- front leg roundhouse kick
- front leg axe kick
- triple alternating roundhouse kick
- jumping turn kick
- back kick
- front leg side step, front leg roundhouse kick
- front leg side step, front leg out-to-in axe kick
- double roundhouse kick
- in place switch stance, rear leg roundhouse kick
- jumping back kick
- front leg feint, front leg roundhouse kick to face
- rear leg feint, front leg jumping axe kick
- front leg roundhouse kick, double roundhouse kick
- front leg feint, rear leg roundhouse kick
- front leg feint, rear leg axe kick
- front leg feint, jumping turn kick
- front leg feint, back kick

b. Kicking Counterattacks

Attack: front leg roundhouse kick
Counter: - slide back, front leg roundhouse kick
            - jumping back kick
            - step back, double roundhouse kick
            - slide back, double roundhouse kick
            - front leg draw, roundhouse kick to face
            - spin whip kick

Attack: rear leg roundhouse kick to face
Counter: - diagonal side step, rear leg roundhouse
            - front leg draw, front leg short axe kick
            - front leg draw, simultaneous rear leg
              jumping roundhouse kick
            - slide back, rear leg short axe kick

Attack: rear leg axe kick
Counter: diagonal side step, rear leg roundhouse kick

Attack: front leg jumping axe kick
Counter: - rear leg step back, front leg roundhouse
            - in place front leg roundhouse kick
            - jumping back kick
            - spin ship kick
            - slide back, front leg roundhouse kick

Attack: jumping turn kick
Counter: - back kick
            - spin whip
            - front leg draw, front leg axe kick
            - rear leg roundhouse kick
            - slide back, double roundhouse kick

Attack: aggressive footwork by opponent
Counter: - front leg short axe kick
            - short slide back, back kick
            - short slide back, rear leg roundhouse kick

Attack: rear leg roundhouse kick (when you switch stance)
Counter: - slide back, rear leg roundhouse kick
                 - slide back, double roundhouse kick
                 - back kick
                 - spin whip kick

2. Open stance

   a. Kicking Attacks

   - rear leg roundhouse kick
   - rear leg axe kick
   - rear leg roundhouse, withdraw, rear leg roundhouse
   - step in, back kick
   - double roundhouse kick

   b. Kicking Counterattacks

Attack: back foot roundhouse kick
Counter: - jumping back kick
                 - spin whip kick
                 - slide back, rear leg roundhouse kick
                 - slide back, double roundhouse kick

Attack: rear foot axe kick
Counter: - slide back, front leg roundhouse kick
                 - back kick
                 - jumping back kick
                 - spin whip kick

Attack: double roundhouse kick
Counter: using footwork, block with arms and attack

In general, taekwondo competition takes place in closed stance or open stance. However, the actual situation in competition varies according to the opponent's footwork, techniques or deceptive strategy. Complex technical strategy requires direct experience of competition and adequate training to be able to adjust to the varying situations that arise in each match. The current trend in taekwondo competition is a preference for launching initiative attacks using the front leg and using safe attacks from closed stance by cutting off the opponent's opportunity to score.

Supplementary Training Methods

There is a variety of equipment that can be used to supplement taekwondo training including the heavy bag, forearm shield, weight jacket, wrist weights, and bicycle inner tubes. The most common items are the target, kicking/punching mitt and jump rope.

1. Target and kicking/punching mitt

The purpose of using the hand held target and mitt for training is to improve accuracy, agility, reflexes and power. Every technique must be performed with full focus and maximum reflexive speed. The competitor should attempt to simulate a realistic attacking kick or punch with every repetition. According to the distance to the target, the competitor must also execute the necessary footwork preceding the attack.

During target training, the types of stances, positions, distance and attacks should be varied regularly for a comprehensive workout. To improve coordination, begin with light and simple techniques and build up to more complex and powerful attacks. It is important to practice both left and right sides equally at each training session.

The target holder should stand in walking stance or modified side stance. The target should be held tightly with the elbow slightly bent. It is the responsibility of the target holder to vary the height, angle, distance and position of the target, so the competitor can practice as many skills as possible. When the competitor begins to tire and concentration wanes, target practice should be stopped.

Benefits of target/mitt training

Fixed target	Moving target	Reflex target
explosive power strength maximum accuracy	agility distance control footwork selection	coordination timing speed

2. Jump rope

Jumping rope is economical because it can be done anywhere, at any time, with minimal cost. It is an excellent method for improving cardiovascular capacity, rhythm, lower body power, balance, timing and flexibility. There are two common ways of jumping rope to achieve these benefits:

a. **six one minute round**s with a one minute break between rounds, varying the speed of jumping throughout

b. **three two minute rounds** with a two minute break between rounds, maintaining maximum speed throughout

When jumping rope, keep the upper body, especially the spine, erect and look straight ahead. Relax the shoulder and arms and keep the upper arms and elbows close to the body. Keep the wrists at waist height and use only the circular motion of the wrists to rotate the rope. Bend the knees slightly to increase the elasticity of movements and jump on the balls of the feet. Jumping can be done on both feet simultaneously or alternating feet, with the rope rotating forward, backward or cross handed.

Training System

The following system provides a ready made framework for developing sparring skills in an intensive, interval training format. Each of the skills is performed in a predetermined pattern while aiming for maximum speed and accuracy of execution. For realism, competitors wear full protection gear and attack and defend in the full contact style of competitive sparring.

To make this training successful, the coach should give a brief explanation and demonstration of the skills. The competitors then execute the techniques according to the coach's signals. Once the basics of these drills are mastered, application and variations can be easily developed and applied in free sparring.

The following patterns should be used:

a. **1:1** (single attack vs. single counter)
Example: From open stance, the attacker executes a rear leg roundhouse kick. The defender counters with a rear leg in-place back kick.

b. **2:1** (double attack vs. single counter)
Example: From closed stance, the attacker executes a rear leg back kick, followed by roundhouse kick. The defender counters with a back step and rear leg axe kick.

c. **1:2** (single attack vs. double counter)
Example: From open stance, the attacker executes a rear leg roundhouse kick. The defender counters with a rear leg back kick and front foot roundhouse kick.

d. **1:1:1** (single attack vs. single counter vs. single recounter)
Example: From open stance, the attacker executes a rear leg roundhouse kick and steps down with his kicking leg in front, changing his stance. The defender counters with a rear leg back kick. The attacker slides back and executes a rear leg roundhouse kick.

e. **2:1:1** (double attack vs. single counter vs. single recounter)
Example: From closed stance, the attacker executes a lead leg roundhouse kick, followed by rear leg roundhouse kick. The defender counters with a back step and rear leg roundhouse kick. The attacker recounters with a rear leg back kick.

f. **1:1:1:1** (single attack vs. single counter vs. single recounter vs. single recounter)
Example: From closed stance, the attacker executes a rear leg roundhouse kick and steps down with his kicking leg in front, changing his stance. The defender counters with a rear leg roundhouse kick and steps down with his kicking leg in front, changing his stance. The attacker recounters with a rear leg roundhouse kick. The defender recounters with a rear leg roundhouse kick.

Competitor Styles

The following list provides tips for competitors of different styles to maximize their strong points.

1. Aggressive competitor
   a. conceal attacking intention
   b. diversify attacking style
   c. attack in combinations with maximum speed
   d. execute each technique accurately
   e. take advantage of attacking/countering opportunities
   f. control the distance by varying your stance

2. Counterattacking competitor
   a. execute diverse initiation techniques
   b. avoid and counterattack with good timing
   c. after the opponent's attack, move close and prepare for counterattacking
   d. the use of front leg is more advantageous
   e. block or avoid, then counterattack

3. Short competitor (against taller opponent)

a. use footwork and feinting to create a chance to attack
b. when the opponent attacks, avoid or use an immediate counterattack
c. use infighting strategy
d. after an attack, close the distance with the opponent

4. Tall competitor (against shorter opponent)

a. be aware of the opponent's quick dash or attack
b. when the opponent attacks, cut the attack with the lead leg kick and then counterattack
c. use long distance strategy
d. use footwork and feinting to create a chance to attack

5. Distance competitor

a. break the opponent's stance
b. confuse the opponent's sense of distance
c. before attacking, incline the upper body and dash in
d. use quick, surprise attacks
e. use side step or back step attacks

6. Strategic competitor

a. use effective competition management skills to win with minimum effort
b. occupy the central area of the ring
c. if the opponent positions himself near the boundary line, use a combination attack to push him out
d. know that when the opponent frequently, intentionally goes near the boundary, he is setting up a counterattack
e. when the opponent positions himself in the corner, execute a combination attack or prepare to counter
f. when the referee says "kyesok" after "kallyo," attack immediately

Mandatory Protection Gear

There are six types of protective equipment required in WTF taekwondo competition:

      a. trunk protector (momtong hogoo)
      b. head protector (mori bohodae)
      c. groin guard (satbodae)
      d. forearm guard (pal bohodae)
      e. shin guard   (daree bohodae)
      f. women's breast guard (yuja kasom bohodae)

The groin guard, arm guard, shin guard and women's breast protector must be worn under the uniform. All competitors also must wear a WTF approved, V-neck taekwondo uniform.

Forearm guard   Shin guard

Two views of a competitor in full protection gear.

Chapter 5:
Planning and
Implementation

Training is a planned and structured process to create a specific stimulus to the body to improve the fighter's competitive ability. The training must be implemented according to proven principles and methodology.

Goal of Training

The goal of training is to bring out the maximum capacity of the physical condition, technical skill and fighting spirit for the competition.

Content of Training

The training plan must be established based on both long term and short term goals. This is accomplished by creating a daily workout plan based on a comprehensive monthly or yearly plan. To produce maximum results, there are three components that must be carefully considered: intensity of training, duration of training and frequency of training. According to the level of the competitor, the following factors must be included in training:

a. physical strength training
- fundamental conditioning
- sport specific conditioning

b. technical training
- accuracy and power of techniques
- advanced skills

c. strategic training
- attack and counterattack
- individual specialty skills
- opponent management

d. willpower training
- meditation
- mental strength training

e. theoretical training
- competition rules

Principles of the Training Plan

There are five principles for developing a training plan:

a. **Balance** - Balanced training includes the general development of strength, endurance, power, agility, coordination, flexibility, fundamental techniques, and mental toughness.

b. **Comprehensiveness** - Comprehensive training means being aware of the task at hand and knowing what method must be used to accomplish it.

c. **Progressiveness** - Progressive training means adjusting the quality and quantity of the training load accurately and incrementally while moving toward more complex skills.

d. **Repetition** - Repetition training means the continuous practice of skills to instill and enhance natural reflexive responses to competition situations.

e. **Individuality** - Individualized training means considering individual condition and specialties and choosing practice skills and intensity accordingly.

Implementation of the Training Plan

Daily training plan

Daily competition training should be done in three 120 minute segments scheduled in the morning, afternoon and evening. This training, intended for elite level competitors, should be organized as follows:

1. **Warm-up** must be done for twenty to thirty minutes to loosen up the joints and improve flexibility.

2. **Core training** lasts eighty to ninety minutes and consists of professional skills and strategies, combination attacks, counter-attacks, and supplementary strength and endurance exercises.

3. A **cool down** period is used to relax the muscles and recover the normal mental condition through stretching and meditation for ten minutes.

Yearly training plan

The yearly training plan must specify a time line for achieving specific goals. There are three stages:

1. The first stage is the **preparation period** in which general physical conditioning and basic skills are developed. The division of the training between conditioning and skill training should be fifty percent for each.

2. The second stage is the **intensification period** in which the focus of training shifts toward thirty percent physical conditioning and seventy percent advanced technical skill development such as the application of kicks, counterattacks, footwork/kicking combinations, speed kicking and agility training.

3. The third stage is the **perfection period** in which the competitor completes the physical conditioning and strives for technical perfection. Training focuses on sixty percent conditioning and forty percent technical training.

Chapter 6:
Taekwondo Fitness

Physical Condition

Physical condition means the physical capacity that is required to complete a specific task. In taekwondo training, physical condition is measured by strength, endurance and coordination. Strength measures the capacity of the muscular system, endurance measures the capacity of the cardiovascular system and coordination measures the capacity of the nervous system.

Strength and Power

Strength is force that is applied in a static condition. The concept of power includes speed and force. Expressed as an equation: *power = force x speed (speed = distance/velocity).*

Therefore, power is the capacity for explosive and forceful execution of a movement by the corresponding muscles. To increase power, speed and force must be enhanced by developing the contraction capacity of the muscles. This is especially important in taekwondo competition where skills must be executed with maximum speed and force to score.

There are two types of training to develop these attributes for taekwondo competitors:

1. **Strength training** - Strength training includes weight training for overall conditioning, muscle specific weight training, isometric exercises and resistance training.

2. **Power training** - Power training is done to enhance muscular speed. Power training includes shadow sparring with light weights, bicycle tube training, target drills, stair running, uphill running, vertical leaping and jumping kicking drills.

Sample Strength and Power Exercises

Strength & Power #1

Drop both legs to the right/left

Raise both legs straight up

Drop both legs directly overhead

Strength & Power #2

Beginner: Raise the trunk
& legs simultaneously

Advanced: Lift the legs and
trunk fully off the ground

Expert: Touch the head to
the knees and hold

Strength & Power #3

Alternately lift the legs while keeping the knees straight.

Strength & Power #4

Raise the feet and upper body simultaneously.

Strength & Power #5

Raise the body using the upper arm, shoulder and back muscles.

Strength & Power #6

Beginning in push-up position, alternately twist to the right/left.

Strength & Power #7

Lean forward, stretching the arms out parallel to the ground.

Drop the upper body and reach backwards through the legs.

Speed

Speed is one of the most important physical attributes in taekwondo competition. It is the ability to move the body or part of the body from one point to another in the shortest possible time. There are several different types of speed that taekwondo competitors must develop including:

- the ability to perform the same technique at the same speed repetitively
- the ability to move from one place to another quickly
- the ability to move the arms and legs with maximum speed without regard for accuracy of movement
- the ability to move a specific part of the body quickly

To enhance speed, the competitor must strengthen the ability to integrate the many parts of the body into one explosive unit.

The most efficient method of speed development is interval training in which taekwondo skills are performed realistically and at top speed. Between these intervals of activity, the competitor must rest sufficiently to recover his physical condition and mental concentration. Some of examples of **interval training** for competitors are:

- 25 to 30 meter sprinting
- vertical jumping, touching both knees to the chest
- explosive kicking or footwork drills
- zigzag running
- shuttle run
- jumping rope
- signal training

Agility

Agility means the ability to change direction or body position quickly and proceed with another action. It is closely related to strength, reflexes, speed, power, coordination and flexibility. Agility is determined by the contraction speed of the muscle and the reflexive speed of the nervous system. It is a critical factor in taekwondo skill performance because every offensive and defensive movement requires quick, complex responses. In competition, the competitor must perform multiple actions in response to the opponent's action. For example, when the opponent attacks, the defender must combine the correct avoiding footwork with a suitable counterattack.

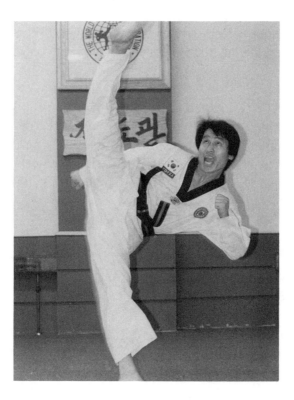

Master Sang H. Kim demonstrates why the ability to move the entire body quickly while performing complex skills is essential in taekwondo.

Sample Speed and Agility Exercises

Speed and Agility #1

Stretch and extend the body while maintaining balance.

Speed & Agility #2

From push-up position, explode upward and clap hands.

Speed & Agility #3

Alternately touch the foot of the extended leg to the opposite hand while looking in the opposite direction.

Strength & Agility #4

Lying on the stomach, alternately touch the foot to the opposite hand.

Speed & Agility #5

Bend forward and touch the hand to the ankle, quickly alternate sides.

Speed & Agility #6

Raise the legs and hips and move the legs in a bicycling motion

Speed & Agility #7

Quickly raise the knee to the chest, alternating sides.

Endurance

Endurance is the ability to maintain an activity for a prolonged period. Endurance depends on the ability of the respiratory system to deliver adequate amounts of oxygen through the blood stream. To improve endurance for taekwondo competition, increase the amount and intensity of training. Some examples of endurance training are:

- running 1,000 meters x 3 sets, with a two minute rest between
- running 100 meters x 5 sets, with a one minute rest between
- sparring 3 minutes x 3 sets, with a one minute rest between
- stair running
- pitching (in-place, alternate knee raises)
- target kicking

Flexibility

Flexibility is the elasticity of the muscles and ligaments. It is a fundamental prerequisite for taekwondo competitors. In general, the degree of flexibility is measured by the range of motion of any technique. The greater the range of motion, the more power that can be generated by muscles. In taekwondo training, it is important to develop good flexibility in the shoulders, waist, knees and ankles.

Stretching is critical for enhancing the range of motion, increasing power and reducing injuries. To maintain flexibility, stretching must be done every day without exception. The best time for flexibility training is after warming-up and after the main training period. The minimum stretching routine for competitors is twice a day for at least ten minutes.

Each exercise should be repeated fifteen times in 3 to 5 sets. Each repetition should be held ten to thirty seconds at the point where the muscle feels stretched slightly beyond comfort. The athlete should continue breathing evenly and naturally throughout the stretching exercises. Generally, breathe out when bending the body and breathe in when erecting the body.

Sample Stretching Exercises

Stretching #1

Alternately lean the body gently to the front and back.

Stretching #2

Rotate the upper body in a circle in both directions.

Stretching #3

Alternately raise each knee to the chest and hold.

Stretching #4

Twist the upper body from side to side.

Stretching #5

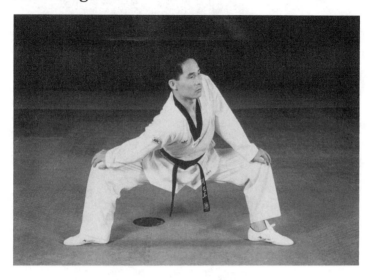

In horse riding stance, twist the upper body from side to side.

Stretching #6

Place one knee on the ground and lean forward gently.

Stretching #7

Begin from a standing position and have your partner slowly lower your body to the ground. (Advanced practitioners only)

Stretching #8

In side kick position, stretch to the front and side.

Stretching #9

With one foot flat on the floor, extend the other leg to the side.

Stretching #10

With the legs outstretched, twist the trunk from side to side.

Stretching #11

Cross one leg over the other and twist the trunk to the rear.

Stretching #12

With one leg outstretched, pull the other foot to the chest.

Stretching #13

Cross one leg over the other and lean forward to touch the toes.

Stretching #14

With one leg bent behind, stretch forward toward the toes.

Stretching #15

With both legs outstretched, reach forward toward the toes.

Stretching #16

Raise one leg up toward the chest while keeping the other straight.

Stretching #17

Kneeling, spread the knees outward and lower the hips.

Stretching #18

Split the legs and lower the body to the ground.

Stretching #19

Spread the legs out to the side and stretch alternately to the center and both sides. Vary the upper body position for the most effective stretch.

Stretching #20

Raise the upper body and look upward.

Stretching #21

Kneeling, reach forward with the arms.

Coordination

Coordination is the ability to quickly and accurately accomplish a task in a variable situation. Coordination is essential for learning new skills easily and adapting them as necessary. There are six components of coordination:

A. responsiveness
B. analysis
C. extrapolation
D. integration
E. transformation
F. differentiation
G. timing

Responsiveness

Responsiveness is the ability to react quickly and appropriately to expected or unexpected sensory cues. It is directly related to competition performance and is highly dependent on the opponent's movements. To improve coordination, the athlete must use physical reflex training drills like attack/counterattack drills and mental toughness training to enhance concentration.

Analysis

Analysis is the ability to observe and evaluate the opponent's reaction to your strategy. This includes discerning the opponent's skill level, strengths and weaknesses, habits, favorite skills, etc.

Extrapolation

Extrapolation is the ability of the competitor to forecast his or his opponent's technical or strategic behavior based on experience and observation. Through extrapolation, the competitor can feint or setup the opponent and estimate his response.

Integration

Integration is the ability to perform accurately and strategically in the constantly changing situation of the competition arena. This can be accomplished by the coordination of total body movement with the movements of the individual arms and legs. The following are the most important components in kicking techniques:
- footwork
- trunk movement (vertical, horizontal or spinning)
- arm movement to use reaction force
- lower body coordination

Transformation

Transformation is the ability to manipulate physical techniques and strategic considerations to take advantage of an unfavorable situation. Some examples of this are:
- transformation from failing to predict the opponent's attack
- transformation from attacking with the wrong technique
- transformation from being setup by the opponent's feint
- transformation from an unfavorable external environment
  (poor conditions, unfavorable spectators, etc.)
- transformation from internal emotional turmoil
  (insecurity, passivity, arrogance, hyperactivity)

Differentiation

Differentiation is the ability to discern a true attack from a feint or setup. Understanding the nature of the opponent's offensive attack allows the fighter to select appropriate counterattacking skills without falling into the opponent's trap. It is also important in developing a keen sense of distance and timing. Differentiation is essential for an accurate and versatile technical performance.

Timing

Timing is the ability to select the best time or speed for performing the proper technique so as to achieve the desired result. It is the most important factor in taekwondo competition for synchronizing the entire body and executing scoring techniques. Timing ability can be measured through reflex time and execution time. It can be improved somewhat through practice and competition experience, but it is generally an innate skill. Some components that enhance timing are flexibility, coordination, strategic thinking, strategic attacking, rhythm, and tempo.

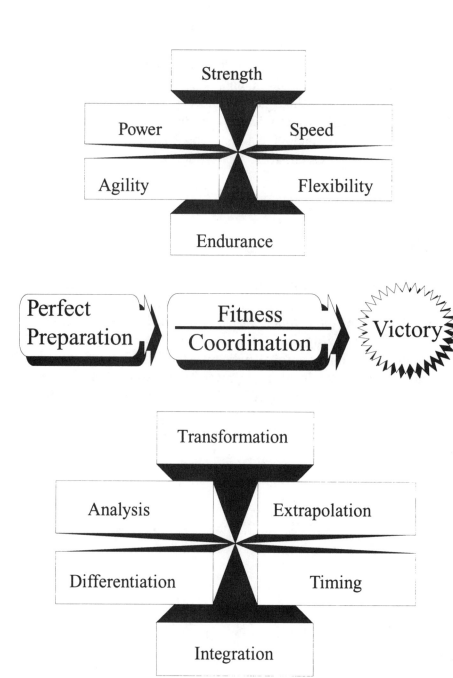

Essential Components of a Taekwondo Athlete

Chapter 7:
Preparation for Competition

The primary goal of training is preparing for competition. During competition, the competitor deploys skills and tactics learned and reinforced in training. Vigorous training must be geared to develop the full capacity of the competitor for optimum performance. Competition is a part of training as well as the training objective. Professional training contributes to developing the athlete's competitive ability and consistency. Therefor, the level of improvement and the effectiveness of training must be evaluated regularly.

Special Preparation

Special preparation for competition must be started at least four to six weeks before the competition date. The goal and content of the special preparation must be identified and established at the outset. This identification process includes analyzing the nature of the competition and the types of opponents anticipated. To carry out the competition preparation plan successfully, the following factors must be considered:

> a. weight control to attain the competition weight
> b. energy management and strategic tactics on a round by round basis
> c. confidence of the competitor
> d. proper warm-up for 10-15 minutes before competition
> e. concentration and fighting spirit

Competition Observation

Competition observation is a method to enhance the effectiveness of the competitive ability. Therefore the data collected must be accurate and statistical. There are three fundamental ways of observing the competition: recording freely on paper, use of an objective form to record observations, and video taping. During the observation, the following things must be measured: the competitor's ability and capacity, the competitor's attitude, and competition management. Based on these observations, the competitor and opponent can be evaluated as follows:

a. **Competitor**
   - analysis and correction of weaknesses and mistakes
   - feedback and enhancements of skill level

b. **Opponent**
   - prompt information analysis as the situation varies
   - analysis of the opponent's weaknesses and errors

The Coach and Competitor

The relationship between the coach and competitor is essential in drawing out the competitor's full potential. There are three basic phases of the coaches duty:

a. Pre-competition

- The coach must assess and prepare for environmental conditions at the competition site.
- The coach must help the competitor finish warming up ten to fifteen minutes before the match.
- The coach must analyze the opponent before the match and provide the competitor with strategic advice.
- The coach must help the competitor to relax and instill confidence in the outcome of the match.

b. During the match

- The coach must analyze the overall competition and the opponent's skill level and give advice to the competitor for the next round.
- During the break between rounds, the coach must revitalize the competitor through breathing exercises and reinforcement of the fighting spirit.
- The advice given between rounds must be simple and to the point.
- The coach must refresh the competitor's physical condition by providing water and towels.

c. Post-competition

- The coach must check the physical condition of the competitor for injuries, anxiety or exhaustion.
- The coach must analyze the results of the competition with the competitor.
- The coach must encourage the competitor regardless of the outcome of the match.
- The coach must help the competitor recover his physical condition and restrengthen his mind set.
- The coach must advise the competitor to cool down adequately then shower with warm water for at least 3 minutes and cold water for 1-2 minutes.

Mental Training

Mental training is the most popular method to enhance the competitive ability in every sport in the world today. It has the potential to enhance physical ability by visualizing the execution of skills. Mental training must be based on the experience and observations of the competitor.

The following **factors** must be considered before any mental training method is applied:

a. Visualization requires abstract thought processes to conceive how the skill should be performed.
b. Actual practice must be considered in mental training.
c. Slow movements are good for image training.
d. The combination of physical training and mental training brings results that last longer than physical training alone.

The **benefits** of mental training are as follows:

a. Mental training shortens the learning period of a skill.
b. Abstract thinking enhances consistency of movement.
c. Mental training improves speed.
d. Mental training reduces injuries.
e. Mental training is an excellent supplement during the warming-up period.
f. Mental training is good for reducing errors/upgrading skills.
g. Mental training improves strategic skills like footwork, counterattacking, etc.
h. In competition, mental training helps performance.

Meditation

Meditation has been known as one of the best mental training methods in martial arts tradition for centuries. It calms the energy level in the body, enhances circulation, improves confidence and strengthens concentration. In taekwondo competition, the competitor must execute accurate techniques with maximum power in constantly changing situations, therefore mental calmness and concentration is absolutely necessary to attain victory.

Meditation can be done sitting with the legs crossed in front of the body and the back straight. Attention should be focused on the danjun, the central area of the body believed to be a well spring of energy located approximately two inches below the navel, and the body should be relaxed. The nose and navel should be aligned on a vertical line. Each breath should be deep, calm and long. Visualize a word or phrase to focus the attention.

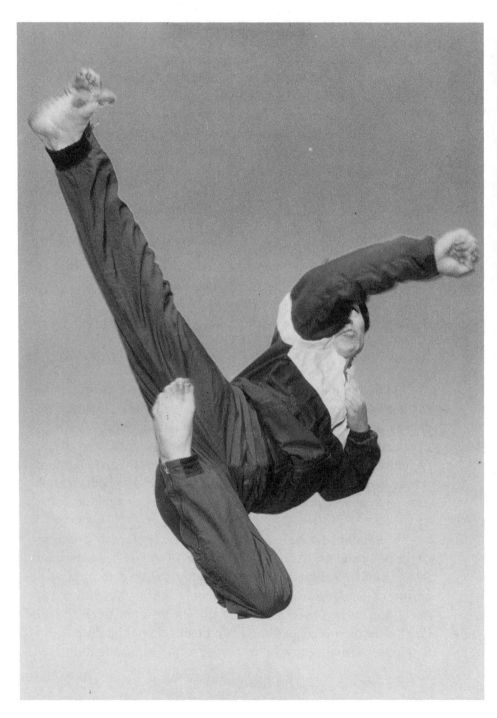

Master Sang H. Kim

Chapter 8:
Sports Medicine

Nutrition

Nutrition is the most important aspect in the management of athletes. Nutrition directly affects the training process and results as well as the ability to compete and recover quickly from competition. Good nutrition can be achieved through daily diet management, including the regulated intake of carbohydrates, fats, protein, vitamins, minerals and water.

Carbohydrates can be obtained through grains, potatoes, pasta, and rice. Carbohydrates enhance endurance because they are digested and absorbed by the body quickly (in about ninety minutes) to provide necessary energy. Carbohydrates should make up sixty percent of the daily diet.

Fat can be obtained through butter, nuts, eggs, and fish. Fat should not make up more than thirty percent of the total daily diet. Fat is a direct energy source like carbohydrates. During intense training, carbohydrates are the main energy source, but in less intense endurance training, fat is the main energy source.

Protein can be obtained through milk, butter, cheese, fish and meat. Protein has fewer calories than fat, but breaks down more slowly in the body (in about four to five hours), making it a long term source of energy.

The average male taekwondo competitor needs 3,500 or more calories depending on the intensity of daily training. However, care should be taken in the meal scheduling to avoid fatigue that follows immediately after meals, especially on days of competition or intense training. On the day of competition, the competitor should eat a high carbohydrate, low protein meal two to three hours before the scheduled match. After intense training or competition, the competitor must eat a high carbohydrate meal to recover the expended energy.

A **sample meal schedule** for competitors:

1. Breakfast   25% of daily intake
2. Snack   10 % of daily intake
3. Lunch   30% of daily intake
4. Snack   10% of daily intake
5. Dinner   25% of daily intake

Tips for eating on the day of competition:

1. Eat a light meal two to three hours before the match
2. During competition, avoid mineral water and sugar based sports drinks. Drink only enough natural water to wet the mouth between matches.
3. Eat lunch one hour after the last match and at least two hours before the next match. If the lunch break is too short, eat bread or fruit as a supplement.

Weight Control

Kyorugi is a competition based on weight classes. The taekwondo competitor should be conscious of his or her optimum weight. Maintaining an ideal weight for his or her physical condition is critical for top performance. The amount of calorie intake during the training period varies according to age, gender, training intensity and duration.

Here are some tips for **daily weight management**:
1. Maintain the optimal weight on a daily basis
2. Use a sauna to sweat off excess water weight
3. Obtain medical advice regarding diet and weight loss
4. Measure and record weight regularly
5. Sweat regularly in daily training

The taekwondo competitor generally wants to compete in the lowest weight division in which he can maintain his physical condition. When the competitor reaches a good weight, he should observe the following cautions to **prevent harmful side effects**:

1. Weight reduction should not exceed more than eight percent of the normal body weight.
2. To reduce weight, the competitor should not sacrifice good nutrition. Eat low calorie but nutritious foods.
3. Adjust the amount of calories carefully during intense training periods.
4. Drink at least one liter of water daily.
5. Take in vitamins and minerals through fruits and vegetables.
6. Do not use drugs or other artificial means to lose weight.

The above advice is for adults only. Children should never attempt to lose weight.

Massage

Massage is very important for competitors. It helps the body to recover from the physical and mental exhaustion of competition as well as stimulate the muscular and nervous systems. Massage can be used during training, and before, after and during competition. Self massage can be helpful, however massage by a trained professional is much more effective.

To perform sports massage, use the finger tips to press points along the nervous system and blood vessels, stroke the length of the muscles or use the palm to press and shake the muscles in a circular motion. Light massage is safer for athletes than deep massage.

There are three stages of massage. The first stage is to pour massage oil or alcohol on the palm of the hand. The second step is to start massaging the specific part of the muscle with the palm. Gradually intensify the pressure. The final stage is to shake the muscle gently and relax. Avoid massaging injured parts of the body. Spend five to ten minutes for each specific area, and thirty to forty-five minutes for the entire massage.

Types of massage

1. **Post-training massage**. Post-training massage is used to promote circulation and to relax the muscles used in training to speed recovery. The best type of post-training massage is deep massage.
2. **Pre-competition massage**. Pre-competition massage is used as part of the warm-up to enhance the circulation and prevent cramps. It should be a light, gentle massage.
3. **Between round massage**. Light massage between rounds should be used to reduce nervousness, speed recovery and prevent injuries. For example, the coach can have the competitor

sit while the coach holds his ankles and shakes his legs slightly. He also can rub the stomach of the competitor lightly or massage the neck and shoulders to reduce tension.

4. **Post-competition massage**. Post-competition massage is used to recover from the fatigue of competition. The massage should be moderate and not painful.

Injuries

Taekwondo is a contact combat sport in which the competitor is always open to the risk of injury. The most frequent injuries are to the toes, instep, knees, hips and arms. The **major causes of injuries** in taekwondo competition are:

1. Technically unprepared competitors
2. Technically mismatched opponents
3. Overconfidence
4. Overanxiety
5. Inexperience
6. Inadequate equipment/facilities

Tips to prevent injuries:

1. Thorough warm-up
2. Maximum concentration during training/competition
3. Follow the directions of the coach and trainer
4. Proper selection and utilization of safety gear
5. Follow the competition rules
6. A medical advisor should always be present during training and competition.

First aid tips for competition:

1. Carefully observe the injured competitor.
2. If the injury is serious, protect and immobilize the injured part.
3. Avoid moving or touching the injured part.

4. Use RICE: Rest, Ice, Compression, Elevation.
5. Respond promptly and calmly.

Equipment necessary for a competitor's **first aid kit:**

1. Cool spray
2. Adhesive bandages and gauze
3. Antibacterial cream or ointment
4. Massage oil or liniment
5. Scissors
6. Tweezer
7. Sling or immobilizing bandage
8. Tourniquet

Fatigue

Fatigue is a phenomenon where lactic acid builds up in the body causing the competitor to feel lethargic and decreasing physical capacity. All sports related fatigue comes from the overexertion of the major muscle groups and the cardiovascular system.

The **effects of fatigue**:
1. Decrease in physical capacity
2. Decrease in judgmental ability
3. Increased risk of injury
4. Increased reflex time
5. Decrease in speed

The coach or trainer must understand the science of training so the competitor can train for maximum results without unnecessary fatigue. After training, the competitor must have adequate rest and take a hot shower to increase circulation. Post-training massage, adequate sleep and good nutrition are also important.

Chapter 9:
Competition Rules

Official Rules of the World Taekwondo Federation, Korea

Article 1. Purpose

The purpose of the Competition Rules is to manage smoothly and fairly all matters pertaining to competitions of all levels to be promoted and/or organized by the WTF, Regional Unions and member National Associations, ensuring the application of standardized rules.

Article 2. Application

The Competition Rules shall apply to all the competitions to be promoted and/or organized by the WTF, each Regional Union and member National Association.

However, any member National Association wishing to modify any part of the Competition Rules must first gain the approval of the WTF.

Article 3. Competition Area

The competition area shall measure 12m X 12m in metric system and have a flat surface without any obstructing projections. The competition area shall be covered with an elastic mat.

However, the competition area may be installed on a platform 50cm - 60cm high from the base, if necessary, and the outer part of the boundary line shall be inclined with a gradient of less than 30 degrees for the safety of the contestants.

1. Demarcation of the competition area
    1) The 8m x 8m area in the inner part of the competition area of 12m x 12m shall be called the Contest Area and the outer part of the Contest Area shall be called the Alert Area.
    2) The demarcation of the Contest Area and the Alert Area shall be distinguished by the different colors of the two areas' surface, or indicated by a line 5cm wide in white color in case the entire surface is one color.
    3) The demarcating line between the Contest Area and the Alert Area shall be called Alert Line and the marginal line of the Competition Area shall be called the Boundary Line.

2. Indication of positions
    1) Position of the Referee
    The Position of the Referee shall be marked at a point 150cm back from the center point of the Competition Area to the opposite side of the Head of Court's seat and designated as the Referee's mark.
    2) Position of the Judges
    The Position of the Judges shall be marked at a point 50cm outwards from each corner of the Boundary Line facing towards the center point of the Competition Area.
    3) Position of the Head of Court
    The Position of the Head of Court shall be marked at least 100cm away from the center of the Boundary Line facing the Referee's mark.
    4) Position of the Recorder
    The Position of the Recorder shall be marked at a point 300cm to the right and 100cm back from the position of the Head of Court.

5) Position of the Commission Doctor

The Position of the Commission Doctor shall be marked at a point 600cm to the side of the position of the Recorder.

6) Position of the Contestants

The Position of the contestants shall be marked at a point 100cm to the left and right sides of the center point of the Contest Area facing towards the position of the Head of Court. The left side shall be the Red Contestant's mark and the right side shall be the Blue Contestant's mark.

7) Position of the Coaches

The Position of the coaches shall be marked at a point at least 100cm away from the Boundary Line of each contestant's side.

8) Position of the Inspection Desk

The Position of the Inspection Desk shall be set up near the entrance of the Competition Area for inspection of the contestants' protective equipment.

Article 4. Contestants

1. Qualification of contestants
    1) Holder of the nationality of the participating team
    2) One recommended by the national Taekwondo Association
    3) Holder of Taekwondo Dan certificate issued by the Kukkiwon/ WTF

2. The Costume for Contestants
    1) The contestant shall wear a Taekwondo uniform (Dobok) and protectors recognized by the WTF.
    2) The male contestant shall wear the trunk protector, head protector, groin guard, forearm and shin guards before entering the contest area and groin guard, forearm and shin guards shall be worn inside the Taekwondo uniform. The female contestant shall wear the trunk protector, head protector, women's groin guard, women's breast guard, forearm and shin guards before entering the contest area, and women's groin guard, women's breast guard, forearm and shin guards shall be worn inside the Taekwondo uniform.
    3) The contestant shall wear the contestant's number on the back of the uniform.

3. Medical control
  1) The use or administration of drugs or chemical substances
     described in the IOC doping bylaws is prohibited.
  2) The WTF may carry out any medical testing to ascertain if a
     contestant has committed a breach of this rule, and any winner
     who refuses to undergo this testing or who proves to have
     committed such a breach shall be removed from the final
     standings.

Article 5. Weight Divisions

1. Weights are divided into Male and Female divisions.
2. Weight divisions are divided as follows:

CATEGORY	MALE DIVISION	FEMALE DIVISION
FIN	Not exceeding 50Kg	Not exceeding 43kg
FLY	Over 50kg & not exceeding 54kg	Over 43kg & not exceeding 47kg
BANTAM	Over 54kg & not exceeding 58kg	Over 47kg & not exceeding 51kg
FEATHER	Over 58kg & not exceeding 64kg	Over 51kg & not exceeding 55kg
LIGHT	Over 64kg & not exceeding 70kg	Over 55kg & not exceeding 60kg
WELTER	Over 70kg & not exceeding 76kg	Over 60kg & not exceeding 65kg
MIDDLE	Over 76kg & not exceeding 83kg	Over 65kg & not exceeding 70kg
HEAVY	Over 83kg	Over 70kg

Article 6. Classification and Methods of Competition

1. Competitions are divided as follows:
  1) Individual competition shall normally be between contestants
     in the same weight class. When necessary, adjoining weight
     classes may be combined to create a single classification.

2) Team Competition
   Systems of competition:
   (1) Five (5) contestants with no weight limit
   (2) Eight (8) contestants by weight classification
   (3) Four (4) contestants by weight classification (Consolidation of the eight weight classifications into four weight categories by combining two adjoining weight classes.)

2. Systems of competition are divided as follows:
   1) Single elimination tournament system
   2) Round robin system

3. All international-level competitions recognized by the WTF shall be formed with participation of at least 3 countries with no less than 3 contestants in each weight class, and any weight class with less than 3 contestants cannot be recognized in the official results.

Article 7. Duration of Contest

The duration of the contest shall be three rounds of three minutes with one minute of rest in male and female divisions. However, the duration of the contest may be shortened to three rounds of two minutes with one minute of rest.

Article 8. Drawing Lots

1. The drawing of lots shall be conducted one day prior to the first competition in the presence of the WTF officials and the representatives of the participating nations, and the drawing of lots shall be done from Fin weight up in the English alphabetical order of the official names of the participating nations.

2. Officials shall be designated to draw lots on behalf of officials of participating nations not present at the drawing.

3. The order of the draw may be changed according to the decision of the Head-of-Team meeting.

Article 9. Weigh-in

1. Weigh-in of the contestants on the day of competition shall be completed one hour prior to the competition.

2. Weigh-in shall be conducted in the nude.

3. Weigh-in shall be made once, however, one more weigh-in is granted within the time limits for official weigh-in to the contestants who did not qualify the first time.

4. So as not to be disqualified during official weigh-in, a scale, the same as the official one, shall be provided at the contestants place of accommodation or at the arena for preweigh-in.

Article 10. Procedures of the Contest.

1. Call for Contestants
The name of the contestants shall be announced three times beginning three minutes prior to the scheduled start of the contest.

The contestant who fails to appear in the contest area within one minute after the scheduled start of the competition shall be regarded as withdrawn.

2. Physical and Costume Inspection
After being called, the contestants shall undergo physical and costume inspection at the designated inspection desk, and the contestant shall not show any signs of aversion, and also shall not bear any materials which could cause harm to the other contestant.

3. Entering the competition area
After inspection, the contestants shall enter into the waiting position with one coach.

4. Start and End of the Contest
The contest in each round shall start with the declaration of "Shijak" (start) by the Referee and shall end with the declaration of "Keuman" (stop) by the Referee.

5. Procedures before the beginning and after the end of the Contest

   1) The contestants shall turn to the Head of Court and make standing bow at the Referee's command of "Charyeot" (attention) and "Kyeong-rye" (bow). A Standing bow shall be made from the natural standing posture of "Charyeot", by inclining forward at the waist to an angle of more than thirty degrees with the head inclined to more than forty-five degrees and the fists clenched at the sides of the legs.

   2) The contestants shall face each other and exchange a standing bow at the Referee's command of "Jwawoohyangwoo" (face each other), "Kyeongrye" (bow).

   3) The Referee shall start the contest by commanding "Joonbi" (ready), and "Shijak" (start).

   4) After the end of the last round, the contestants shall stand at their respective positions facing each other and exchange a standing bow at the Referee's command of "Charyeot", "Kyeongrye", and then shall turn to the Head of Court and make a standing bow at the Referee's command of "Jwawoohyang-woo", "Kyeongrye", and wait for the Referee's declaration of the decision in a standing position.

   5) The Referee shall declare the winner by raising the winner's hand according to the result of the contest. However, when the winner is unable to stand at his/her position due to injury, the Referee shall declare the winner by raising his/her own hand on the winner's side.

   6) Retirement of the contestants.

6. Contest Procedures in Team Competition

   1) Both teams shall line up in column in the submitted team order facing the Head of Court.

   2) Procedures before the beginning and after the end of contest shall be conducted as in Item 5 of this Article.

   3) Both teams shall leave the Contest Area and stand by at the designated area for the turn of each contestant's match.

   4) Both teams shall line up in the contest area immediately after the end of the final match facing each other.

   5) The Referee shall declare the winner by raising his/her own hand to the winning team's side.

Article 11. Permitted Techniques and Areas.

1. Permitted techniques
    1) Fist techniques: Delivering techniques by using the front parts
       of the forefinger and middle finger of the tightly clenched fist.
    2) Foot techniques: Delivering techniques by using the part of the
       foot below the ankle bone.

2. Permitted areas
    1) Trunk
    Within the limits of the area from the horizontal line at the base
      of the Acromion down to the horizontal line of the Iliac crest,
      attack by fist and foot techniques are permitted. However, such
      attacks shall not be made on the part of the back not covered
      by the trunk protector,
    2) Face
    This area is the front part of the face on the basis of a coronal line
      at both ears, and attack by foot technique only is permitted.

Article 12. Valid Points

1. Legal scoring areas
    1) Midsection of the trunk: The abdomen and both sides of the
       flank
    2) Face: The permitted parts of the face

2. Points shall be awarded when permitted techniques are delivered
accurately and powerfully to the legal scoring areas of the body.
However, when a contestant is knocked down as a result of the
opponent's attack on a part of the trunk protector which is not a part
of a legal scoring area, such a technique shall be regarded as a point.

3. Each scoring technique shall earn 1 (plus one) point.

4. Match score shall be the sum of points of the three rounds.

5. Invalidation of points
 When the following are committed, the delivered technique will not

be scored:
1) Intentionally falling, immediately after delivery of the legitimate technique.
2) Committing an illegal act after delivery of the legitimate technique.
3) Use of any of the prohibited actions.

Article 13. Scoring and Publication

1. Valid points shall be immediately recorded and publicized.

2. In the use of protectors not equipped with electronics, valid points shall be immediately marked by each judge by using an electronic scoring instrument or judge's scoring sheet.

3. In the use of electronics protectors
1) Valid points scored on the midsection of the trunk shall be recorded automatically by the transmitter in the electronic trunk protectors.
2) Valid points scored to the face shall be marked by each judge by using the electronic scoring instrument or judge's scoring sheet.

4. In case of scoring by using the electronic scoring instrument or judge's scoring sheet, valid points shall be the ones recognized by two or more judges.

Article 14. Prohibited Acts

1. Penalties on any prohibited acts shall be declared by the referee.

2. In the case of multiple penalties being committed simultaneously, the heavier penalty shall be declared.

3. Penalties are divided into Kyong-go (warning penalty) and Gam-jeom (deduction penalty).

4. Two Kyong-gos shall be counted as deduction of one (1) point. However, the last odd Kyong-go shall not be counted in the grand total.

5. A Gam-jeom shall be counted as minus one (-1) point.

6. Prohibited acts: Kyong-go penalty
    1) Grabbing the opponent
    2) Pushing the opponent with the shoulder, body, hands or arms
    3) Holding the opponent with the hands or arms
    4) Intentionally crossing the Alert Line
    5) Evading by turning the back to the opponent
    6) Intentionally falling down
    7) Pretending injury
    8) Attacking with the knee
    9) Attacking the groin intentionally
    10) Intentionally stomping or kicking any part of the leg or foot
    11) Hitting the opponent's face with hands or fist
    12) Gesturing to indicate scoring or deduction by raising hand, etc
    13) Uttering undesirable remarks or any misconduct on the part
        of the contestant or the coach.

7. Prohibited acts: Gam-jeom penalty
    1) Attacking the fallen opponent.
    2) Intentional attack after the Referee's declaration of Kalyeo
    3) Attacking the back and the back of the head intentionally
    4) Attacking the opponent's face severely with hands or fist
    5) Butting
    6) Crossing the Boundary Line
    7) Throwing the opponent
    8) Violent or extreme remarks or behavior on the part of the
        Contestant or the coach

8. When a contestant refuses to comply with the Competition Rules or the Referee's order intentionally the Referee may declare the contestant loser by penalties.

9. When the contestant receives minus three points the Referee shall declare him/her the loser by penalties.

10. Kyong-go and Gam-jeom shall be counted in the total score of the three rounds.

Article 15: Decision of Superiority

1. In the case of a tie score by deduction of points, the winner shall be the contestant awarded any point or more points through the three rounds.

2. In case of a tie score other than Case 1 above, where both contestants received the same number of points and/or deductions, the winner shall be decided by the Referee based on superiority through out all three rounds.

3. Decision of superiority shall be based on the initiative shown during the contest.

Article 16. Decisions

1. Win by K.O.
2. Win by Referee stopping the contest (RSC)
3. Win by score or superiority
4. Win by withdrawal
5. Win by disqualification
6. Win by Referee's punitive declaration

Article- 17. Knock Down

1. When any part of the body other than the sole of the foot touches the floor due to the force of the opponent's delivered technique.

2. When a contestant is staggered showing no intention or ability to pursue the match.

3. When the Referee judges that the contest cannot continue as the result of any powerful technique having been delivered.

Article 18. Procedures in the Event of a Knock Down

1. When a contestant is knocked down as the result of the Opponent's legitimate attack, the Referee shall take the following measures;

   1) The referee shall keep the attacker away from the downed contestant by the declaration of "Kalyeo" (break).
   2) The Referee shall count aloud from "Hanah" (one) to "Yeol" (ten) at one second intervals towards the downed contestant, making hand signals indicating the passage of time.
   3) In case the downed contestant stands up during the Referee's count and desires to continue the fight, the Referee shall continue the count up to "Yeodul" (eight) for recovery of the downed contestant. The Referee shall then determine if the contestant is recovered and, if so, continue the contest by declaration of "Kyesok" (continue).
   4) When a contestant who has been knocked down cannot demonstrate the will to resume the fight by the count of "Yeodul", the Referee shall announce the other contestant winner by K.O.
   5) The count shall be continued even after the end of the round or the expiration of the match time.
   6) In case both of the contestants are knocked own, the Referee shall continue counting as long as one of the contestants has not sufficiently recovered.
   7) When both of the contestants fail to recover by the count of "Yeol", the winner shall be decided upon the match score before the occurrence of the knock down.
   8) When it is judged by the Referee that a contestant is unable to continue, the Referee may decide the winner either without counting or during the counting.

2. Procedures to be followed after the contest.
Any contestant suffering a knock-out as the result of a blow to the head will not be allowed to compete for the next 30 days. Before entering a new contest after 30 days, the contestant must be examined by a medical doctor designated by the National Taekwondo Federation, who must certify that the contestant is recovered and able to compete.

Article 19. Procedures for Suspending the Match

When a contest is to be stopped due to injury of one or both of contestants, the Referee shall take the following measures;
1) The Referee shall suspend the contest by declaration of "Kalyeo" and order the Time Keeper to suspend the time keeping by announcing "Kyeshi."
2) The Referee shall allow the contestant to receive first aid within one minute.
3) The contestant who does not demonstrate the will to continue the contest after one minute, even in the case of a slight injury, shall be declared the loser by the Referee.
4) In case resumption of the contest is impossible after one minute, the contestant causing the injury by a prohibited act to be penalized by Gam-jeom shall be declared the loser.
5) In case both of the contestants are knocked down and are unable to continue the contest after one minute, the winner shall be decided upon points scored before the injuries occurred.
6) When it is judged that a contestant's health is at risk due to losing consciousness or falling in an apparently dangerous condition, the Referee shall suspend the contest immediately and order first aid to be administered. The Referee shall declare as loser, the contestant causing the injury if it is deemed to have resulted from a prohibited attack to be penalized by Gam-jeom or, in the case the attack was not deemed to be penalized by Gam-jeom, shall decide the winner on the basis of the score of the match before suspension of the time.

Article 20. Referees and Judges

1. Qualifications
Holders of International Referee Certificate registered by the WTF.

2. Duties
1) Referee
   (1) The Referee shall have control over the match.
   (2) The Referee shall declare Shijak", "Keuman" "Kalyeo", "Kyesok" and "Kyeshi", winner and loser, deduction of points, warnings and retiring. All the Referee's declarations shall be made when the results are confirmed.

(3) The Referee shall have the right to make decisions indepen-
    dently in accordance with the prescribed rules.
(4) The Referee shall not award points.
(5) In case of a tied or scoreless match, the decision of superiority
    shall be made by the Referee after the end of three rounds.
2) Judges
    (1) The Judges shall mark the valid points immediately.
    (2) The Judges shall state their opinions forthrightly when
        requested by the Referee.

3. Responsibility for judgement
Decisions made by the Referees and Judges shall be conclusive and
they shall be responsible to the Board of Arbitration for those
decisions.

4. Uniform of the Referees and Judges
    1) The Referees and Judges shall wear the uniform designated by
       the WTF.
    2) The Referees and Judges shall not carry or take any materials
       to the Arena which might interfere with the contest.

Article 21: Head of Court.

1. Qualification
Holder of International Referee certificate with years of experience
in competition management.

2. Duties
    1) Overall control and supervision of the pertinent competition area
    2) Confirmation of the decision
    3) Evaluation of the Referee's and Judges' performance
    4) Giving a report at any meeting of the Board of Arbitration

Article 22. Recorder
The recorder shall time the contest and periods of time-out
suspension and also shall record and publicize the awarded points
and/or deduction of points.

Article 23. Assignment of Officials

1. Composition of officials
    1) In the use of non-electronic trunk protectors: The officials are composed of one Head of Court, one Referee and four Judges.
    2) In the use of electronic trunk protectors: The officials are composed of one Head of Court, one Referee and two Judges.

2. Assignment of officials
    1) The assignment of the Head of Court, the Referees and Judges shall be made after the contest schedule is fixed.
    2) Referees and Judges with the same nationality as that of either contestant shall not be assigned to such a contest. However, an exception shall be made for the Judges when the absolute number of the Referees and Judges is wholly insufficient.

Article 24. Other matters not specified in the Rules

In the case that any matters not specified in the Rules occur they shall be dealt with as follows:

1. Matters related to the competition shall be decided through consensus by the Head of Court and the Refereeing officials of the pertinent contest.

2 Matters which are not related to a specific contest shall be decided by the Executive Council or its proxy

Article 25. Arbitration

1. Composition of Board of Arbitration
    1) Qualifications: Member of Executive Council of WTF or person of sufficient taekwondo experience recommended by WTF President or Secretary General.
    2) Composition: One Chairman and less than six members.
    3) Procedures of appointment: The Chairman and members of the

Board of Arbitration will be appointed by the WTF President on the recommendation of the WTF Secretary General.

2. Responsibility: the Board of Arbitration shall make corrections of misjudgments according to their decision regarding protests and take disciplinary action against the officials committing the misjudgment or any illegal behavior and the results of which shall be sent to the Secretariat of the WTF.

3. Procedures of protest
    1) In case there is an objection to a judgement, a delegate must submit an application for reevaluation of decision (protest application) together with the prescribed fee to the Board of Arbitration within 10 minutes after the pertinent contest.
    2) Deliberation of reevaluation shall be carried out excluding those members with the same nationality as that of either contestant concerned and resolution on deliberation shall be made by majority.
    3) The members of the Board of Arbitration may summon the Head of Court and refereeing officials for confirmation of events.
    4) The resolution made by the Board of Arbitration will be final and no further means of appeal will be applied.

4. Other provisions
A video tape recorder shall be set up at each court for deliberation of the protest.

SUPPLEMENTARY PROVISION

These Competition Rules shall come into force from October 7, 1990.

Appendix A:
Taekwondo Competition
Terminology

A

apchook	ball of foot

B

badah chagi	counter kicking
bal	foot
balbadak	sole of foot
baldung	instep
bal jitgi	footwork
banguh	defense
bankyug	counterattack
baro	return to ready stance
bikyu jitgi	side step
boosang	injury
booshim	corner judge

C

chagi	kick
chajumpyo	judging paper
charyut	attention
chegup	weight division
chung	blue
chung sung	blue wins

D

datchimsae	closed stance
dobok	uniform
dollyu chagi	roundhouse kick
doobal dangsung	double kick
dui chagi	back kick
duihooryu chagi	spin whip kick
duikoomchi	heel
dukjum	point

H

hoejun	round
- il hoejun	first round
- ee hoejun	second round
- sam hoejun	third round
hogoo	chest protector
hong	red
hong sung	red wins
hooryu chagi	whip kick

J

jayoo kyorugi	free sparring
jirugi	punch
joonbee	ready
jooshim	referee

K

kalyeo	break
kamdokkwan	head of court
kamjum	deduction point
keoman	end
kibon	basic
kihap	yelling
kikwon	withdrawal
kisool	technique
- kibon kisool	basic technique
- junmoon kisool	professional technique
kongkyuk	attack
- kanjup kongkyuk	indirect attack
- jikjup kongkyuk	direct attack
- kiooru kongkyuk	incline attack
- danil kongkyuk	single attack
- mikurro kongkyuk	sliding attack
- jejari kongkyuk	in-place attack
kudup chagi	continous kicking
kulro jitgi	sliding step
kyesok	continue
kyorugi	sparring

kyorumsae	fighting stance
- ap kyorumsae	front fighting stance
- yup kyorumsae	side fighting stance
- ohrun kyorumsae	right handed stance
- woen kyorumsae	left handed stance
kyunggi	competition
kyunggijang	competition site
kyunggi kyuchick	competition rules
kyunggo	warning
kyungrye	bow
kyunggye seon	boundary line

M

machuo kyorugi	arranged sparring
makki	block
- momtong makki	middle section block
- arae makki	low section block
- ulgool makki	high section block
moollu jitgi	back step

N

naeryu chagi	axe kick
naga jitgi	forward step
natchoomsae	low stance

P

panjung	decision
pihagi	avoiding

S

satbodae	protection cup
shigan	time
shihap	competition
shijak	begin
shilkyuk	disqualification
shimpan	judge

W

woosae	superiority

Y

yullimsae	open stance

Appendix B: References

Kukki Taekwondo Kyobon	Kukkiwon	Kukkiwon	1989
International Referee text	WTF	WTF	1992
Sport Theory & Application	Daegun Kim	Sunil Pub.	1988
Elite Sports Training	Hongwon Chae	Bokyng Pub.	1992
Coaching Theory	Jeyun Ku	Hyungsul Pub.	1991
Taekwondo Kyorugi	Yungryul Choi	Samhak Pub.	1989
Taekwondo Quarterly	KTA	KTA	1993
Training Methodology	Jonghoon Kim	Kyohak Pub.	1990
Training Theory	Jimwon Kim	Donghwa Pub.	1988
Living Meditation	Heesun Park	Jungshin Pub.	1992
Sportmassage	BfLW	Wien	1986
For MVP	Mansoo Kang	B & R	1992
Teaching: Way of the Master	Sang H. Kim	Turtle Press	1991
Ultimate Fitness	Sang H. Kim	Turtle Press	1993
Trainingslehre	Harre		1986
Grundlagen des Sportlichen Trainings	Matwejew	Sportverlag	1977
Boxsport	Horst Fiedler	Sportverlag	1980
Judo	Gerhard Lehmann	"	1983
Fechten	Berndt Barth	"	1979
Rinjen	Jurgen Hartmann	"	1980
Leistungssteuerung	M. Grosser	Sportwissen	1986
Konditionstraining	M. Grosser	"	1981
Techniktraining	M. Grosser	"	1986
Riktig Taekwondo	Kyong M. Lee	BLM	1987
Taekwondo	Kyong M. Lee	Alma Press	1989

About the Authors

Kuk Hyun Chung

Master Kuk Hyun Chung, considered by many to be the greatest taekwondo competitor ever, won the Gold Medal in Taekwondo in the 1988 Summer Olympic Games. He is listed in the *Guiness Book of Sports Records* as winning the most World Championship titles (1987, 1985, 1983, 1982) by a single person and is undefeated in International Competition. He also won the Athlete's Award in 1984 and 1983 for outstanding performance in competition. He is a graduate of the Korean National College of Physical Education. His latest achievement is the leading role in the 1994 action movie "Taekwon Fighter."

Kyung Myung Lee

Grandmaster Kyung Myung Lee is currently the Deputy Secretary General of the World Taekwondo Federation, headquarters of taekwondo in Seoul, South Korea. He is a 9th degree black belt and author of 5 martial arts books in German, Korean, and Polish. He was the 1988 Olympic coach for the Austrian Olympic Taekwondo Team and chairman of the Technical Committee of the European Taekwondo Association. He is a graduate of Yonsei University.

Sang H. Kim

Master Sang H. Kim is an internationally respected author of 5 martial arts books, including the best sellers *Ultimate Fitness through Martial Arts* and *Teaching: the Way of the Master*, and star of over 35 martial arts instructional videos. He won the 1976 Korean National Champion and was named Instructor of the Year in Korea in 1983. He holds an M.S. degree in physical education from Southern Connecticut State University and currently devotes his time to teaching and presenting martial arts seminars for students and instructors.

Index

NOTES

Other books from Turtle Press

Teaching: The Way of the Master
Combat Strategy
The Art of Harmony
Rape Awareness and Prevention
Advanced Teaching Report
Ultimate Fitness through Martial Arts
Launching a Martial Arts School

For more information:
Turtle Press
PO Box 290206
Wethersfield CT 06129-0206
Phone: 1-800-77-TURTLE